# THE DESCENDANTS

OF

# *John Stubbs*

OF

## CAPPAHOSIC
### GLOUCESTER COUNTY
### VIRGINIA

# 1652

## William Carter Stubbs, Ph.D.

### HERITAGE BOOKS
2026

# HERITAGE BOOKS

### *AN IMPRINT OF HERITAGE BOOKS, INC.*


## Books, CDs, and more—Worldwide

For our listing of thousands of titles see our website
at
www.HeritageBooks.com


A Facsimile Reprint
Published 2026 by
HERITAGE BOOKS, INC.
Publishing Division
5810 Ruatan Street
Berwyn Heights, MD 20740

International Standard Book Number
Paperbound: 978-1-55613-429-6

# INTRODUCTION.

*To the Members of the Stubbs Family:*

This little pamphlet is printed for private distribution only. A copy will be presented to each member of the family, with the hope that after a close examination a report will be made of all errors, either of omission or commission, to the undersigned for correction in the next edition.

The author is painfully aware of its imperfections, but it is the best that he could *extort* from the various branches of the family after the expenditure of much time and labor. On account of apathy and indifference, his letters of inquiry were frequently unanswered; hence the incompleteness of several lines. His thanks are due, however, and are hereby tendered to several members for the valuable assistance given him.

While conscious of the incompleteness of his work, the author is yet emboldened to publish what he has, realizing that the information contained herein is too valuable to be withheld from print. He hopes in the future to publish a revised and more complete edition, and will do so at an early day if every member of the family will assist in making the necessary corrections and amendments.

Whatever the merits of this little pamphlet may be, it is given to the family with the modest hope that it may stimulate each and every member to nobler deeds and higher aspirations.

WILLIAM CARTER STUBBS,

*Audubon Park, New Orleans, La.*

# INDEX.

# PREFACE.

In writing of the Stubbs family every effort has been made to secure all the information possible, both in England and America. There is accordingly given, first, a chapter embodying "gleanings" that have been gathered from various sources in England, mainly, however, from a delightful little volume, "The Lays and Leaves of the Forest" (of Knaresborough), by Rev. Thos. Parkinson—whose mother was a Stubbs.

The next chapter is devoted to the early settlers by the name of Stubbs in America, with their land grants, etc.

The remainder of the pamphlet is devoted to the descendants of John Stubbs of Cappahosic, the earliest immigrant to Virginia (about 1652), who is believed to be the ancestor of all the Southern Stubbses.

William Carter Stubbs

# CHAPTER I.

## THE ORIGIN OF THE FAMILY OF STUBBS

is by common consent located in the Forest of Knaresborough, Yorkshire, England. This Royal Forest of Knaresborough is a range of country about twenty miles in length and eight in width, diversified with mountain and moor, rocky eminences and fertile valleys, and extending from Knaresborough westward and southwestward to the heather-clad hills overlooking Bolton Abbey. Originally it was a wild and rugged district with rich, heavily-wooded valleys, and uplands covered with ferns and heathers, a place admirably adapted as a refuge for the superstitions of the old British and Saxon creeds. In mediæval times it was surrounded by feudal strongholds and ecclesiastical establishments of the first magnitude. Later the lowlands were enclosed and cultivated, but wide, wild uncultivated tracts of great extent remained open and unclaimed until the end of the Eighteenth Century, when by Act of Parliament it was enclosed.

Modern times have completely changed the original scenes, and to-day nothing remains of the Forest but its name. The town of Leeds has taken possession of the Washburn valley and transformed it into a chain of reservoirs to supply water to the city. An obscure hamlet has risen into a fashionable, world-famed town of Harrogate, where healing waters and bracing breezes attract the invalid from every clime. Eugene Aram, Blind Jack of Knaresborough and the famous Mother Shipton are some of the local characters and celebrities of this Forest.

In this Forest originated many of the families whose names are familiar to us all. The Yorkshire Archæological Society has recently published a roll for the whole county of Yorkshire, taken from the rolls of the King's Exchequer of the names who paid a subsidy or tax to the King in the second year of King Richard II. (June, 1378, to June, 1379). The text is in Latin, but can be easily translated. In this list are many familiar names—some in their primitive spelling, indicating their origin. Here are some of them: Richard Wil-son (that is, Richard, the son of Wil); Thomas Atkyns-son, Adam Alice-son, Richard Nelle-son, Agnes Nelle-doghter, John de Beckwith, William del Hall, William del West, John Cowhird, Richard Carter, Richard Lyster (Lister, *i. e.*,

Richard the Dyer), Agnes Parcour (the park keeper, now Parker), Richard Polayn (now Pullein, a forest name derived from "Pullus," a colt given to the keeper of the Royal stud), William Stubbe (the ancestor at an early date of the late illustrious Right Rev. William Stubbs, Bishop of Oxford), William de Thakwra (a name made famous by his descendant William Makepeace Thackeray), Elias Moor-house, Richard Schiphird (*i. e.,* Sheep-herd, now Shepard), Thomas del Holme (*i. e.,* of the "holm" or flat land by the water, now Holmes), Margaret Webster (a trade name, a weaver), Robert Fflesshewer (a flesh cutter or butcher, now Fletcher).

Besides the above may be found the familiar names of Legitt, Hudson, Banks, Simpson, Swynton, Deen, Brewstir, Colyer, Johnson, Robynson, Scott, Moss, Hill, Gyll, Neusom, Turpyn, Taillour, Young, Wright, Milner, Boller, Bland and others.

From a poem called "The Hunt," given in "The Lays and Leaves of the Forest" (of Knaresborough), by the Rev. Thomas Parkinson, the following verses are selected:

> "John Jeffrey of 'The Trees' is there,
>   And Stubbs of Whitewall Nook—
> Guy Palmes of Lindley th' sport to share
>   Hath come o'er moor and brook."
>
> *        *        *        *        *        *
>
> "But oft a root though hid away
>   By *shoot* is not unknown,
> And Fairfax, Stubbs and Thackeray
>   Are names the world doth own."

The Stubbses were then foresters from the Royal Forest of Knaresborough. As before mentioned, in the subsidy roll of the second year of Richard II. (1378-1379), for the Villa de Clynt, occurs the entry, Willelmus Stubbe et uxor:

"The home of William Stubbe and his wife was at Birstwith, then included in Villa de Clynt."

William was probably the first who bore the name of Stubbe. The name was not fixed fifty years afterward, as his grandsons were still called "de Stubbe" or "Stubbes." The name is thought to be derived from "stob" or "stub," the root end of a broken tree. Such an object may have existed in the vicinity of the family residence, and hence the members would receive the designation "de," *i. e.,* of Stubb or Stubbs. (See "Lay and Leaves of the Forest," by Rev. Thomas Parkinson.)

The Yorkshire Archæological Society's Journal mentions that "about 1350 A. D. flourished Thomas de Stubbes, or Stubs, who was born in Yorkshire and entered the order of Black Friars at York and became a Master of Theology. He was remarkable for ecclesiastical learning and religious life. He was ordained Priest

Dec. 20th, 1343, A. D., in Durham Cathedral, but the date of his death is unknown. From his learned pen fourteen valuable works proceeded."

From a sketch of the ancestry of the late Bishop William Stubbs of Oxford, it appears that—

"William Stubbe of 1379 A. D. had a son also named William, and his son, John de Stubbes, in 1430 was an officer,—the Grave of the Forest of Knaresborough. John de Stubbes' son, William Stubbes, resided at Ripon, but John de Stubbes' property at Birst-with descended in 1442 to William's son Thomas. This Thomas was followed in succession by his son, also named Thomas, in 1490. This second Thomas was also 'Grave of the Forest,' and therefore had probably returned to the residence at Birstwith in 1498. His brother, William Stubbs, was chaplain in 1516 to the Shepherd Lord Clifford of Skipton and Barden. Thomas Stubbs died in 1535, and his son and successor, Miles Stubbs, died in 1555. Miles left two sons—William, the elder, married Alice Belton and went to reside at Felliscliffe; John, the other brother, also resided at same place. William of Felliscliffe died in 1575. His third son was Thomas Stubbs, who resided at Whitewall and died there in 1648, aged 75 years. Thomas the son of Thomas of Whitewall was connected by marriage with the Atkinsons, who held one of the principal farms under the Ingilby family of Ripley at Haverah Park, and between 1664 and 1672 he succeeded Thomas Atkinson there as tenant. His son, Thomas Stubbs, born 1650, married Alice Simpson of Clint and died in 1716.

"Though tenants on the farm of Haverah Park the family was of substantial yeoman rank, owning considerable property in the neighborhood. The eldest son of Thomas, and his successor on the farm, was John Stubbs, who had numerous descent. The fourth son of Thomas was Joseph Stubbs, who broke away from the family home and resided at Graystone Plain in Felliscliffe. He had three sons—Thomas, Joseph and William—who resided in London and from whom descended the Rev. Stewart Dixon Stubbs, vicar of St. James's, Pentonville. Thomas Stubbs, the eldest son, born in 1735, removed to Ripley and thence he or his descendants successively to Boroughbridge and Knaresborough, where, in the last generation, the family occupied the position of wine merchants, bankers and solicitors. At Knaresborough in 1825 the great-grandson of Thomas Stubbs of Ripley was born, Bishop William Stubbs, the subject of this article."

A study of the pedigree of Bishop Stubbs will show many branches unaccounted for. It is suggested by one of our English cousins that a son of John, the son of Miles above, went to London

and may be the progenitor of the John Stubbs who came early to
Virginia. In a recent letter to the writer from Rev. Charles William Stubbs, D. D., Dean of Ely, given below, mention is made of
Stubbses in later times in Shropshire, Suffolk and London.

In 1620 "Mr. Stubbs" bought of Mr. Thomas Maddox for £25
two shares in the Virginia Company of London. Mr. Stubbs was
also member of the London Company in London in 1622 (Brown's
Genesis of U. S., page 940). That a descendant of this Mr.
Stubbs came to Virginia and settled is highly probable.

In Burke's General Armory we find "Lawrence Stubbs and
Richard Stubbs' (1525) arms in the chapel Balliol College, Oxford." (Vist. Oxon. 1574.)

"Sa. on a chevron engrailed between in chief two lilies and in
base a pheon ar. three leopards' faces az. a chief gu. charged
with two keys saltirewise between as many trunks of trees eradicated and couped or. pierced through with arrow of the second."

The coat of arms as given by our English cousins is described
as follows:

"Field of shield azure, with bend in gold upon which are three
buckles in sable. Upon the field are stags' horns with an arrow
head above them. The stag's head above is the same which Edward I. of England used upon his coat of arms.

The motto is *Aequo adeste animo* (Be of just mind).

Arms: Az. on a bend or. between three stag's horns pierced with
arrows, three buckles sa.
   Crest: A stag's head.
   Motto: Aequo adeste animo. *Be ye ready with unruffled courage.*

The following is a copy of letter received from Rev. Charles William Stubbs, D. D., Dean of Ely:

"DEANERY ELY, 24th MAR., '02.

"*My Dear Sir*—There is little doubt, I think, that Knaresborough Forest is the original home of the Stubbs, the village of Fewston and its neighborhood not far from the Harrogate being its centre. My grandfather, who at one time lived at New Hall, a substantial yeoman farmer and corn factor, close to Fewston, and the family may be traced back steadily to the time of Richard II., when William Stubbe, 1379, is found on the roll. In 1430 his grandson, John de Stubbes, was "reeve" of the Forest of Knaresborough, so on down through the centuries, Johns, Williams, Thomases, for the most part. There are Stubbses also in later times to be found in Shropshire, Suffolk and London. In this neighborhood one of the oldest of the Norman families, the Le Stranges, married an Alice Stubbs of Ledgeford, and I saw the other day over the old Inigo Jones gateway carved the arms of Sir Harmon Le Strange quartered with those of his wife. The Stubbs arms of course you know. The Stubbs type of build and face is, I fancy, very persistent. Bishop Stubbs and myself trace back to a common ancestor two centuries, but our friends have said there was a distinct family likeness, especially of coloring. The habit of blushing pretty late in life is a noticeable trait and one of which I at least do not choose to be ashamed. A son of the Shropshire stock whom I knew in Liverpool was possessed of the same physical heredity.

"Historically I suppose we may be proud of Thomas the Dominican Monk of York; Historian Philip Stubbs, author of Anatomy and Malady; John Stubbs, the Puritan pamphleteer; George Stubbs, the great horse painter.

"If I come to America again, as I may possibly do next winter, we must try to meet. I need hardly say that if you are in England I shall be glad to welcome you here.

"Cousinly yours,
"CHARLES W. STUBBS."

## ILLUSTRIOUS MEMBERS OF THE FAMILY.

Biographical dictionaries contain accounts of several Stubbses who have become famous. Allusion has already been made to Thomas the Dominican Monk; to the late Right Rev. William Stubbs, D. D., LL. D., Bishop of Oxford; to the Rev. Charles W. Stubbs, D. D., Dean of Ely, and to Rev. Stewart Dixon Stubbs, D. D., Vicar of St. James.

Another distinguished minister was John Stubbs, who, according to Fox's Journal, was a very zealous itinerant Quaker preacher. He traveled extensively in England, Scotland, Ireland, Wales and Holland. He was a man of great literary attainments and was one of those who out of thirty languages paved the way of "thee" and "thou" as the words with which to address a single person. He finally came to America with Fox, and seems never to have returned.

In the legal and political world two distinguished representatives of the Stubbs family are found.

First, John Stubbs, an English lawyer and Puritan, born 1540. He wrote a pamphlet against Queen Elizabeth's marriage with the Duke of Anjou, entitled "The Discovery of a Gaping Gulf Wherein England is Like to be Swallowed by Another French Marriage," and was condemned to lose his right hand. The sentence was carried out and the intrepid lawyer raised his cap with the other hand and said, "God save the Queen."

Second, Henry Stubbs was a great English scholar and writer, born in 1631, in Lincolnshire. He joined the party of Cromwell during the civil war and wrote "A Vindication of Sir Harry Vane," "Light Shining Out of Darkness," and other works. After the restoration he went over to the royalists and published numerous attacks upon his former friends. He was accidentally drowned in 1676.

George Stubbs, born 1724 in Liverpool, was a very distinguished painter. Possessed of an extensive knowledge of anatomy, he excelled in delineating animals, particularly horses. He published in 1766 a treatise on "The Anatomy of the Horse." His picture of the "Grosvenor Hunt" is esteemed a masterpiece. He died in 1806.

But the most distinguished member of the family, past or present, was the great prelate and historian, to whom frequent mention has already been made, Bishop William Stubbs of Oxford, whose death recently occurred. Born at Knaresborough in 1825 and educated at Christ Church, Oxford, he became a fellow of Trinity and was ordained in 1848. He became Regius Professor of History at Oxford in 1866, Bishop of Chester in 1884, and

Bishop of Oxford in 1888. He was author of many works. His work, "The Constitutional History of England," is acknowledged the world over as a standard authority. He was nominated on behalf of the Crown in 1879 by the late Earl of Beaconsfield to the canonry. The graceful act on the part of the Premier was received by all parties with much favor as the recognition of great erudition and untiring industry, and merited the encomium of the "Review" as being equally to the honor "of him who gave and him who took."

BISHOP STUBBS married, 1859, Catherine Dellar of Naverstock and had issue:

(1) William Walter, b. 1866, now Assistant Master at Dalwich College; (2) Launcelot Henlock Ascough, b. 1869; (3) Lawrence Morley, b. 1874; (4) Wilfred Thomas, b. 1875; (5) Reginald Edward, b. 1876; (6) Katherine Isabella, b. 1863.

# CHAPTER II.

Mention has already been made of the purchase by Mr. Stubbs of Mr. Thomas Maddox for £25 two shares of the Virginia Company of London, Nov. 13th, 1620. He was also a member of the London Company in 1622. Probably John, the son of this man, settled in Virginia, as the old court records show a John Stubbs in Virginia in 1671. It is highly probable that John patented lands in Virginia as early as 1652, since we find on the land books at Richmond that John repatented 300 acres, patented by William Roberts in 1652 and subsequently escheated to the commonwealth. In this patent, given below, this land adjoined the lands of said Stubbs, because in "its metes and bounds" it mentions one of them as the said *"Stubbs spring."* It is believed that this John or his father patented before this a large tract adjoining this (Roberts') tract, since he was possessed later of a large area. He also, in 1706, obtained the escheated lands of Christopher Webster, 150 acres. In 1703 he patents 50 acres (1 head right) betwixt the lands of Augustine Warner, Mr. Woll and William Bolling, in another part of the county, now a part of White Marsh ("Stubbs"). The records of Gloucester county, Virginia, were destroyed in 1820 and again during the late civil war, and hence the absence of valuable information concerning the early settlers of this county. The land books at Richmond and the records of Petsworth and Abingdon Churches in Gloucester county are the chief sources of information at this early date.

Here are the copies of the patents from the land books at Richmond:

"In 1652 William Roberts patents 300 acres of land on the N. side of York River and N. W. side and at ye mouth of Jones Creek, bounded as follows: South up Jones Creek, east upon a white marsh, north upon the lands of Ed. West upon York River." (Vol. X., page 214.)

This land was escheated to the commonwealth and in 1714 John Stubbs repatented it, and it is thus described on the Land

Book, Vol. X., page 537: "In Petso (Petsworth) parish, Gloucester county, Virginia, beginning on Jones Creek and running along a gut, and thence on south side to the mouth of said gut, and thence N. W. to an ash tree, and thence to a holly bush in a white marsh, and thence N. 80° to a small pine and hickory standing near the branch, and on, crossing the head of Fleming's little creek, and then N. E. 74 poles, etc., to the marsh of said creek, and thence south near to the said *Stubbs'* spring, and thence S. to York River, and thence down the river 104 poles to the beginning."

This land adjoined the land upon which the original home of John Stubbs was located, and since all of this section was patented about 1652, soon after the opening of the county to settlers, it is highly probable that John Stubbs originally patented his home tract about the same time that William Roberts did the escheated tract.

In 1703 John Stubbs patents 50 acres (1 Head right, John Maytor) in Abingdon parish, Gloucester county, Virginia, betwixt the lands of Augustine Warner, Mr. Woll and Wm. Bolling. Vol. IX., page 535.

In 1702 John Stubbs patents 150 acres, viz.: "Christopher Webster's escheated land as per William Jones, deputy of Mathew Pope, escheator of same county, and a jury sworn before him for that purpose, 15th May, 1701, John Stubbs, of County of Gloucester, hath made composition, etc., this 25th May, 1702. ffr. Nicholson, Gov."

These lands were situated on York River and Jones Creek, and included the Cappahosic tract, together with "Valley Front" and "Concord" (formerly Mulberry Hall), now owned by the writer. John Stubbs "the younger," in 1786, sold Cappahosic out of the family. It was repurchased by the father of the author in 1852, and by him sold in 1868. "Valley Front" and "Concord," parts of the original tract, are still held in the family. At "Valley Front" is situated the old home, and here, too, is the burying ground of the Stubbses.

In the old General Court records of Virginia occurs a suit in 1671 between John Stubbs and Richard Moore, with "Lawrence Smith and Richard Booker appointed by court to adjust the differences."

In the York records in 1672 is a suit of John Stubbs vs. William Gilbert.

In 1698-99 and '02 the names of John and Richard Stubbs occur several times.

In 1702 Richard Stubbs was arrested by John Young for debt, and, said Young not prosecuting, was discharged. This is the last time that his name is found in Virginia.

It may be mentioned here that in 1704 a Richard Stubbs is among the petitioners for a court in the precinct of Neckham, in County of Bath, North Carolina (N. C. H. & G. Reg., Vol. I., No. 3, page 162). It is almost certain that this Richard moved from Gloucester county, Virginia, to Bath county, North Carolina, and became the ancestor of all of the North and South Carolina Stubbses, as will be shown later.

From the Abingdon parish record the following are taken:

"Sus [anna] dau. of John and Susannah Stubbs, b. Aug. ye 9th, 1678.

Mildred, dau. of Capt. John and Eliz'th Smith, b. April, 1699.

John, son of John and Mildred Stubbs, b. May ye 8th, 1722.

Francis, son of John and Mildred Stubbs, b. February ye 21st, 1724.

Elizabeth, daughter of John and Mildred Stubbs, born January ye 29th, 1726.

Peter, son of John and Mildred Stubbs, b. February ye 12th, 1728.

Mildred, daughter of John and Mildred Stubbs, b. February ye 17th, 1731.

Thomas, son of John and Mildred Stubbs, b. November ye 28th 1733.

William, son of John and Mildred Stubbs, b. February ye 1st, 1735.

Lawrence, son of John and Mildred Stubbs, b. September ye 16th, 1738.

Mildred, daughter of John and Jane Stubbs, b. October ye 12th, 1748.

Mary Amiss, daughter-in-law John Stubbs, Jr., died October ye 7th, 1750."

Besides the above there are baptisms of slaves: from 1702 to 1714, belonging to "Mrs. Stubbs;" from 1714 to 1718, belonging to "Mrs. Susannah Stubbs;" from 1723 to 1740, belonging to "Mr. John Stubbs;" from 1740 to 1747, belonging to "Capt. John Stubbs." Also, in 1747, slaves belonging to "Mr. John Stubbs, Jr."

## PETSWORTH PARISH.

The records of births, marriages and deaths having been lost, the following is gleaned from the Vestry Book:

"John Stubbs, Jr., Surveyor of Highways in 1701.

John Stubbs, Surveyor of Highways in 1703-1705.

John Stubbs, Processioner of Third precinct 1709-1719.

John Stubbs dies in 1719.

Thomas Stubbs, with many others, "protests against transubstantiation" in 1714.

Thomas Stubbs, Sheriff of Gloucester county in 1734.

Thomas Stubbs, Processioner Fourth precinct in 1743.

Thomas Stubbs, member of vestry 1745 to 1762.

Thomas Stubbs, dead in 1762.

Capt. John Stubbs, member of vestry 1748-1760.

Capt. John Stubbs, dead in 1760.

Francis Stubbs, Processioner Second precinct 1741.

John Stubbs, Jr., Processioner Sixth and Second precincts, 1751-1759.

Francis Stubbs, member of vestry 1753-1767.

Francis Stubbs, dead in 1767.

Peter Stubbs, lands Fourth precinct, 1755.

Peter Stubbs, Processioner Third precinct 1784.

Francis Stubbs, Processioner Second precinct 1759.

Thomas Stubbs, Processioner Second precinct 1767.

John S. Stubbs, Processioner Second precinct 1784.

From 1753 to 1760 Thomas, Capt. John and Francis Stubbs were members of the vestry together.

From the Commissioner of Revenue's books in Richmond, Va., the following assessments were made for 1782 in Gloucester County, Va.:

John S. Stubbs, 462 acres.

Francis Stubbs' estate, 536 acres.

William Stubbs' estate, 18 acres.

Peter Stubbs, 71 acres.

Lawrence Stubbs, 75 acres.

The military records in Richmond show that—

Capt. John S. Stubbs received 4,000 acres of land.

Midshipman John Stubbs, 1,333 1-3 acres, warrant for which was given October 26th, 1847, to John Bespritch, Eliza Beveridge, Read Purcell and James Purcell, only heirs of John Stubbs, deceased.

Francis Stubbs, 100 acres, private warrant issued May 21st, 1783.

Benjamin Stubbs, 100 acres, warrant delivered to Christopher De Graffenried, assignee, through John Hobson, attorney, June 16th, 1814.

Stubbs Allen, 200 acres, issued to him 23d March, 1784.

Stubbs Allen, 100 acres, to Samuel Brooking, assignee, 23d August, 1784.

### STUBBSES IN PENNSYLVANIA.

Allusion has been made to John Stubbs, a distinguished Quaker preacher, who came to America with Fox and seems never to have returned. This was 1671-1673. Whether this John was the ancestor or a relative of the Thomas who married, in 1721, Mary Minor, in Chester county, Pennsylvania, is unknown to the writer. They were both Quakers. Hon Jesse Stubbs, at a reunion of the Stubbs family in West Elkton, Ohio, August 28th, 1895, gave the genealogy of the descendants of this couple. He claims that this Thomas (died 1763) came from England to America in 1718; that he married, in Chester county, Pa., Mary Minor (who was from Ireland though of English parents) in September, 1721. They had nine children, viz.: Daniel, Esther, Thomas, John, Joseph, Mary, Elizabeth, Sarah and Ann. The descendants of these children are now found scattered all over the Union.

John, the fourth child, moved from Pennsylvania to North Carolina in 1755, and married Esther Maddocks (also of Pennsylvania), daughter of Joseph Maddocks, in 1757 or 1758. To this couple were born fourteen children, six of whom were born in North Carolina, viz.: Nathan, Isaac, John, Mary, Samuel and Esther. In 1768 they removed to Georgia, about thirty miles from Augusta, where the rest of their children were born, viz.: Hannah, Joseph, Rachel, Thomas, Deborah, Sarah, Jesse and William. John died December 27th, 1803, and Esther Maddocks Stubbs in 1786, both in Georgia. All of the children (except one, Sarah, who died young,) married in Georgia. After the death of their father they all moved to Ohio (1804 or 1805) and settled in the southwestern part, along and near Elk Creek, and all lived until 1828. The descendants of John Stubbs are widely scattered throughout the West and Northwest and are thought to be greater in number than those of his brothers and sisters. His total number of grandchildren were ninety-two, great-grandchildren nearly 500, and great-great-grandchildren will probably reach 1,500 or 2,000. (This was in 1895.)

In a letter from Hon. Lewis D. Stubbs of Richmond, Indiana, he says:

"Samuel (above), born May 10th, 1766, died July 28th, 1846, was my grandfather, and he married, January 5th, 1791, Mary Jones. The issue of this union was ten children, of whom my father (born November 13th, 1807,) was the only survivor. He married also a Jones who came from Georgia. One of my brothers was a member of the Eleventh Ohio Volunteer Infantry during the war between the States, first as sergeant, then captain of his company, and finally rose to the rank of Lieutenant Colonel; was at Chickamauga, Atlanta, etc. Joel Cloud of Georgia married one of my grandfather's sisters, and I have often heard from my grandfather of his brothers and sisters, that all their relatives had moved away from the South except one Joel Cloud, who lived near Wrightsboro, Ga. One or more brothers of John Stubbs went to North Carolina and afterward to Georgia, as I understand, about the same time that John went, but their descendants also moved to Ohio about 1804 or 1805 and lived near Mount Pleasant. There are a number of the Stubbs family living in Lancaster county, Pa. They are farmers and in possession of large estates. Some of them are prominent citizens and have occupied important positions."

A letter from President J. E. Stubbs, now of Reno, Nevada, says:

"My father, an only son, was born in the city of Middleton, Pa. His grandfather (Thomas) came from England and settled in that State. My father moved to Ashland, Ohio, in 1840. The family roll call is as follows:

"J. D. STUBBS AND WIFE, Ashland, Ohio.

"Mrs. Elizabeth Dorland, eldest child, Ashland, Ohio.

"D. D. Stubbs, O. & O. Steamship Line, San Francisco, Cal.

"J. C. Stubbs, Vice-President Southern Pacific Railway Company, San Francisco, Cal.

"J. E. Stubbs, President University of Nevada, Reno, Nevada.

"Mary N. Stubbs, Ashland, Ohio.

"W. G. Stubbs, C. O. & T. Co., San Francisco, Cal."

Hon. George W. Stubbs, attorney-at-law, Indianapolis, Ind., whose son, Dr. George W. Stubbs, has recently settled in Crowley, La., writes:

"My grandfather, Jesse (see above), who was next to youngest child of John and Esther (Maddocks) Stubbs, settled just across the line from Ohio in Indiana when he moved from Georgia."

I am informed that Mr. D. E. Stubbs of Eaton, Ohio, is col-

lecting information for a history and genealogy of the descendants
of Thomas and Mary Minor.   This branch of the Stubbs family
in America will, therefore, be dismissed with the above brief re-
cital, given to explain who were those Stubbses whose names are
so frequently found in the early records of Georgia.

# CHAPTER III.

## STUBBS FAMILY OF VIRGINIA AND THE SOUTH.

Although it is believed that a son of the Mr. Stubbs who bought of Mr. Thomas Maddox the two shares of the Virginia Company in 1620, settled in Virginia about 1652, there are no official records known to prove it. The first official record occurs in 1671. From that time on the name of *John Stubbs* occurs frequently in the court records, land books and church registers.

Our official records of births begin in the Abingdon parish register in 1678, with Sus [anna], the daughter of John and Susannah Stubbs. After this date occur in records the names of Richard, Thomas, John and Francis Stubbs, presumably the sons of John and Susannah Stubbs.

Richard apparently left the State in 1703 and probably went to Bath county, North Carolina (see page 20).

Thomas signs the protest, with others, in the vestry book of Petsworth parish, against transubstantiation in 1714, was Sheriff of Gloucester county in 1735, member of vestry of Petsworth from 1745 to his death, in 1762.

John (afterward Captain) was a member of the vestry of Petsworth from 1748 to his death, in 1760.

Francis was processioner in Second precinct in 1741 and member of the vestry of Petsworth from 1753 to his death, in 1767.

The Petsworth vestry book mentions the death of John Stubbs in 1719. It is believed that he was the husband of Susannah and father of the four boys given above, and the ancestor of all of the Stubbses of the South. By being called John, Jr., in 1701, it is probable that he was the son of John the immigrant and perhaps the grandson of the shareholder in the London Company (1620-1622).

### STUBBSES OF NORTH CAROLINA.

Mention has already been made of Richard Stubbs, the son of John and Susannah Stubbs. This Richard appears in the York records between 1698 and 1702 as plaintiff and defendant in several suits. In the latter year John Young has him arrested for debt, and, failing to prosecute at the time, the said Richard is discharged. His name does not occur subsequently in the Virginia records.

In 1704 Richard Stubbs was among the petitioners for a court in the precinct of Neckham, in the County of Bath, North Carolina. (Vol. I., No. 3, page 162, N. C. H. & G. Reg.)

The will of Thomas Stubbs, dated January 17th, 1738. proved March 7th, 1738, mentions sons William, Thomas, Bassett (?) (Everitt), John and Richard, and daughters Hannah and Mary. (N. C. H. & G. Reg.) This Thomas Stubbs evidently married Mary Everitt, as per following deeds:

Thomas Stubbs and wife Mary, April 14th, 1722, a conveyance to Nathaniel Everitt, 100 acres land near Morattucks bridge, adjoining lands of Benjamin Blount. Witnesses, William Rodes and Cornelius Callahan.

Nath. Everitt to Thomas Stubbs, a conveyance of same land, with same witnesses. (Chowan County Deeds, Book C, No. 1, in N. C. H. & G. R., Vol. II., page 144.)

The will of Richard Stubbs, Jr., of Tyrrell county, N. C., February 25th, 1754, mentions brothers Everitt, William, Thomas and John; Ann Jones, sister Mary and my two other sisters; brothers Thomas and Everitt, executors; testators, Esther Walker and Mary Stubbs. (Vol. I., No. 4, page 486, N. C. H. & G. R.)

John Stubbs, in 1749, witnesses will of John Green in Bladen county.

Will of William Stubbs of Bath, December 8th, 1756, proved in Beaufort county 14th June, 1757, mentions son William, wife Jean and daughter Margaret and makes them executors; teste, John Alderson, Samuel Thompson and Peter Caila, (N. C. H. & G. R.)

William Stubbs, in 1751, attests will of Seth Pilkinston of Beaufort county, N. C. (Ibid.)

William Stubbs, member of jury of Tyrrell county, 1739.

William Stubbs appointed sergeant-at-arms by House. 1746.

Thomas Stubbs member of jury of Bath county, 1725.

Legacy of Matthew Rowan of New Hanover, April 17th, 1760, to John Stubbs, son of James Stubbs of Bath county.

William Stubbs and Jean Cullen were married December, 1733, in St. Thomas parish, Beaufort precinct.

From the above, taken from the North Carolina records as given in North Carolina Historical and Genealogical Register, it would appear that Richard had at least two sons, Thomas and James.

(I.) THOMAS married Mary Everitt and had

(1) William, (2) Thomas, (3) Everitt, (4) John and (5) Richard (d. 1754, s. p.), and (6, 7 and 8) three daughters, one probably born after death of father.

(1) WILLIAM married, 1733, Jean Cullen and had William and Margaret.

(2) THOMAS occurs in the records of Tyrrell county in an affidavit against the tory, Thomas Harrison, July 14th, 1777, and may be the Thomas above, son of Thomas.

Nothing is known of Everitt and John, though the occurrence to-day of the name of Everitt in one of the Georgia branches of the Stubbs family would suggest a descent from Everitt.

(II.) JAMES, the second son of Richard, had at least one son, John, living in 1760. Probably this John, or John the son of Thomas, obtained, in November, 1753, a grant of land on Catfish Creek, Peedee River, South Carolina, who, according to Bishop Gregg's History of South Carolina, was the ancestor of all the Stubbses since known in the Marlboro district, South Carolina.

Hon. Harry W. Stubbs, State Senator, of Williamston, Martin county, N. C., writes that his father was Jesse Rolin Stubbs, who married, March 3d, 1868, Mary W. Badham, in Chowan county; that Jesse was the only son of Martin Stubbs of Bath and moved to Martin county in 1857 or 1858.

The above information is given with the hope that it may stimulate some one in North Carolina to continue these investigations.

### THE STUBBSES OF SOUTH CAROLINA.

Bishop Gregg, in his "History of the Old Cheraws," says: "John Stubbs, November, 1753, obtained a grant of land on Catfish Creek, Peedee River, and was the ancestor of the Stubbses since known in the Marlboro district."

This John came from North Carolina and is believed to be a son of James of Bath county and grandson of Richard who went to North Carolina from Virginia, 1703, and who was a son of John and Susannah Stubbs of Gloucester county, Va.

Rev. J. A. W. Thomas, in his History of Marlboro county, S. C., says that "Jno." married Rebecca Conner and had issue.

I. LEWIS, married Elizabeth, daughter of William Bridges, a Lieutenant in Marion's Brigade of the Revolution. Issue:

(1) Rev. Campbell Stubbs, a Baptist minister of Bennettsville, S. C., 1829-1837, and was the grandfather of Mrs.

B. A. Capel, William H. Stubbs and Wyriott J. Stubbs, and late Albert Stubbs of Marlboro county, S. C.

(2) John J., student at University of North Carolina 1822, and is believed to be the father of (a) Tristam Stubbs, who moved to Mississippi, the father of George W. of Dallas, Texas, and Hon. J. J. Stubbs, attorney-at-law, Raleigh, N. C.; and (b) ———, who was the father of Thomas H. Stubbs of Lillian, Miss.

(3) Lewis E., student at University of North Carolina 1822, Ordinary of Marlboro county, S. C., 1835; married daughter of Darby Sweeny.

II. JAMES, married ——— Fuller; issue:

(1) John, married Anne McDonald, originally from Granville county, S. C.; issue:

(a) John W. (b. 1802, d. 1884), married Elizabeth Pate (b. 1809, d. 1873), daughter of Col. Thoroughgood Pate and granddaughter of Col. Pate of the Revolution. She was also a granddaughter of Charles Bright. (For issue see forward page.)

(b) Alexander.

(c) Jackson, b. 1815, still living, hale and hearty; married Anna Bright, granddaughter of Charles Bright; no issue.

(a) Lizzie, d., married Herbert Smith, (d.) 92 years old.

(e) Anna, d., married Uriah Hodge, d.

(f) Lucinda, married John Mason, d.

(2) David.

(3) Alexander, perhaps father of A. A., (C. S. A.), d. 1893.

(4) Silas.

(5) Elizabeth, married Holden Liles, and had James, B. J. and Joseph R. Liles.

(6) Mrs. Pearson.

(7) Mrs. John M. Miller.

(8) Celia, married George Bristow and is the mother of Capt. A. E. Bristow of Bennettsville, S. C.

III. ALEXANDER, d., married Lucy, daughter of Daniel and Martha (Pearce) Sparks; no issue. She married, second, Thomas Stubbs.

IV. THOMAS, married widow of Alexander Stubbs, *nee* Lucy Sparks, and had issue:

(1) Thomas E., married Ann (d. 1895), daughter of James and Deborah (Bethea) Spears.

(2) Benjamin.
(3) John.
(4) Lucy, married E. W. Goodwin.
(5) Rebecca, married Peter Hubbard, and moved to Mississippi.
(6) Feribe, married William Hubbard.

V. WILLIAM, married Elizabeth Hubbard; issue:
(1) James (Big Jim).
(2) Peter.
(3) William F., of McFarland, Anson county, N. C., b. 1804 and still living.
(4) Frances, married Benjamin Moore, Sr. (b. 1769, d. 1846), and had numerous descendants.

VI. JOHN, married Mary, daughter of William Bridges. She was afterward the fifth wife of John David.

VII. PETER.

The following are the children of John W. (b. 1807, d. 1884) and Elizabeth (Pate) Stubbs (b. 1809, d. 1873):
(1) Mary (d.), married Thomas A. Stubbs (d.), a relative.
(2) John B. (Co. F, 21st Regt. S. C. Vols., C. S. A.), farmer of Brightsville, S. C., married Ann Covington, daughter of Col. John Covington.
(3) Ann (d. 1876), married Tom Jones.
(4) Martha F. (d.), married L. G. Pate, a prominent merchant of Sumter county, S. C., and had a son (d.) 5th May, 1902), a minister of South Carolina Conference, M. E. Church, South, and a D. D.
(5) Thoroughgood P. (Co. F, 21st Regt. S. C. Vols., C. S. A.), farmer of Brightsville, S. C., member House of Representatives 1870-1871; married Sallie McRae, granddaughter Ed. Deberry, M. C. from North Caroline in the forties.
(6) James L. (Sergeant Co. B, 24th Regt. S. C. Inf., C. S. A.), a farmer of Leslie, S. C.; married Lou Pearson.
(7) Samuel F. (member Co. F, 21st Regt. S. C. Vols., C. S. A.); captured at Fisher and died at Elmira, N. Y., while a prisoner.
(8) Derrick D. (Corporal Co. F, 21st Regt. S. C. Vols., C. S. A.), a farmer of Brightsville, S. C.; married Esther Chance.
(9) Campbell E. (Co. F, 21st Regt. S. C. Vols., C. S. A.); wounded at ———), a merchant and insurance agent at

Sumter, S. C.; married, first, Alice Hoyt; issue: (a) Hoyt; (b) Reba; (c) Alice; (d) Elvin; married, second, Kate Wood, daughter Rev. Henry M. Wood, M. E. Church South; issue, Allston, b. 1882.

(10) Laurence D., a farmer of Brightsville, S. C.; married Virgie Webster.

(11) Letitia; married W. J. McRae.

The following, taken from History of Marlboro County, will show the Stubbses in C. S. A.:

Lucius Stubbs, Co. K, 8th Regt. S. C. Vols.; died in Richmond, Va., 1861; buried in Bennettsville, S. C.

James, Co. G, 23rd Regt. S. C. Vols.; wounded at Petersburg, and still lives.

John, Co. G, 23rd Regt. S. C. Vols.; killed at Antietam, Md.

Joel, Co. G, 23rd Regt. S. C. Vols.; died during war.

D. D., Co. F, 21st Regt. S. C. Vols., 4th Inf. Corp; captured; living.

C. E., Co. F, 21st Regt. S. C. Vols.; wounded; living.

J. B., Co. F, 21st Regt. S. C. Vols.; captured; living.

M. W., Co. F. 21st Regt. S. C. Vols.; mortally wounded at Petersburg, 1864.

S. F., Co. F, 21st Regt. S. C. Vols.; captured at Fisher; died in prison.

T. E., Co. F, 21st Regt. S. C. Vols.; discharged; died since war.

T. P., Co. F, 21st Regt. S. C. Vols.; discharged; living.

A. A., Co. F, 21st Regt. S. C. Vols.; discharged; died 1893.

J. L., Co. B, 24th Regt. S. C. Inftry.; 3rd sergeant; living.

Thos., Co. B, 24th Regt. S. C. Inftry.

Daniel, Co. B, 24th Regt. S. C. Inftry.; wounded and discharged, 1863.

Thos. A., Co. E, 4th Regt. S. C. Cavalry; dead.

L. D., Co. D, 3rd Regt. S. C. State Troops, Junior Reserves.

Of the above, several are not placed in the account just given. Doubtless they can properly assign themselves. Unfortunately the information relative to the living members of the family in South Carolina is extremely limited. Further data earnestly solicited.

STUBBS FAMILY IN VIRGINIA.

## Descendants of Thomas and Mildred Stubbs.

Allusion has already been made to Richard, Thomas, John and Francis as the probable sons of John, (d. 1719) and Susannah Stubbs, of Gloucester county, Virginia. The descendants of Richard, as far as known, have been given. Thomas, the next brother, married Mildred, presumably a Smith, since the name of Smith has been quite common among his descendants. At "Point Lookout," in Robins' Neck, Gloucester county, Virginia, the old burying ground of the Robins, occurs the following epitaphs:

"In memory of Frances Robins, daughter of Thomas and Mildred Stubbs, born 14th February, 1745, died 18th July, 1800."

"In memory of Thomas Robins, son of William and Elizabeth Robins, born 1st February, 1745, died 8th November, 1808."

"To our father, Thomas Robins, son of Thomas Robins and Frances Stubbs, born January 7th, 1770, died September 18th, 1821."

John Stubbs, the brother of Frances, married Elizabeth Robins, sister of Thomas Robins above, according to will of William Robins (1782), probated 1786, in which are mentioned the children of said union. As far as is known Thomas (d. 1762) and Mildred Stubbs had at least two children:

(1) FRANCES (b. 1745, d. 1800), married Thomas Robins (b. 1745, d. 1808) of Point Lookout. (See Robins excursus for issue.)

(2) JOHN (dead in 1782), married Elizabeth Robins, daughter of Wm. and Elizabeth (Coleman) Robins; issue:
  (a) Thomas (b. 1761, d. 1783 s. p.)
  (b) William (b. *circa* 1763) married and had perhaps at least one daughter, Harriet, who married Thomas Coleman. (See further on page 37.)
  (c) Samuel N. (b. 1765, d. April, 1845) married Mary W. Stubblefield, who died September 4th, 1826, and had issue seven children.

I. Sallie married Joseph De Neufville and had Joseph, married ——, and has two daughters and a son living in New York.

II. Mary married Booker and had a son living in Richmond·

III. Fanny married, first Clark and second Caruthers, and moved to Missouri, and died s. p.

IV. Samuel married Mary Simcoe—lived in New York and had issue:

(1) John (d. s. p.); (2) Frances, married, first, Deboe, and had Mary, who married McDougal of New York; married, second, Richard Jones of Virginia, and had Ella, who married Hamilton of South Orange, N. J., and have two children.

V. Simon Stubblefield, lawyer, member of Legislature, and former mayor of Norfolk City, married Lizzie Shepard and had issue:

(a) Fanny, unmarried.

(b) Kate, unmarried.

(c) William G., married and has one child.

(d) Louisa D., married Wm. Earle of Queen Anne county, Md., and has Fannie, Swepson and William.

(e) Eliza, married Mr. Keeling, of Norfolk, and has Rogers and Martin (both single), and Lizzie, married Lee Hamilton of Accomac county, Va., and Mary, married Allen Cleaveland of Baltimore, Md.

(f) Solomon S., married Mary Brown of Washington, D. C., and has Fannie J., married Mr. Niel of Wyoming, and has Mary, Laura and William.

(g) Alice, married Mr. Joiner.

VI. John Smith (b. 1811, d. 1883), graduate William and Mary College, lawyer in Portsmouth, married Stella Louise Hodges Armistead and had issue:

(a) Annie Wright (d. 1883), married Col. William H. Stewart (C. S. A.) of Portsmouth, and had Robert Armistead, Ph. D., University of Virginia, now a member of its faculty.

(b) Mary Stella, married Rev. William Gould Witherspoon Woodbridge, D. D., Presbyterian minister of Griffin, Ga.; issue, William Witherspoon.

(c) Robert Armistead (b. 1847, d. 1868 s. p.)

VII. Thomas, went West in early life and nothing known of him.

(d) James Coleman (d. 1821, s. p.)

(e) John Smith (d. 1821), married Mary Cooke, and had issue:

I. Elizabeth, married, first, Creamer, no issue; second, Taylor, and had a daughter, who married Mr. Eastwood of Urbanna, Va.

II. John Smith (d. s. p.)

III. Franklin (d., s. p.)

IV. Simon (d., s. p.)

(f) Elizabeth, married Regensburg and had:

I. Samuel (d. 1902), married Miss Fary and had:

 (a) Gertrude, married Powhatan R. Stubblefield; issue, (1) Pocahontas Pearl, (2) Jesse, (3) Annie.

 (b) Cora, married Charles Pierce, and has issue.

 (c) Hattie, married Monroe Pierce, and has issue.

 (d) ———, married Thomas Pierce, and has issue.

 (e) Capilola, married Hudgins, and has issue.

 (f) Samuel, married Lyall.

 (g) William, married Lawson.

 (h) John, married Edwards.

## Descendants of Capt. John and Mildred (Smith) Stubbs.

Capt. John Stubbs, the son of John and Susannah Stubbs, married Mildred Smith, daughter of Capt. John and Elizabeth (Cox) Smith, and granddaughter of Major Lawrence Smith of Bacon's Rebellion, and had issue:

(A) JOHN (b. May 8th, 1722, died July 12th, 1773), married May 9th, 1747, widow of James Amiss, *nee* Jane Segar (b. 1720, d. 1792), and had issue:

I. Mildred (b. October 12th, 1749), married Rev. Thomas Hughes, and had issue:

 (1) Fannie, unmarried, a famous school teacher.

 (2) Charlotte, unmarried, a famous school teacher.

 (3) Sarah Mynn (b. 1774, d. 1864), married, 1809, in St. John's Church, Richmond, Wm. Montague (b. 1774); issue:

 (a) Capt. Thomas Ball (C. S. A.), born 1818, died 1874; married, first, Sarah Ann Jones, and, second, Mrs. Mary B. Jones, *nee* Pollard.

 (b) Charles Wortley (C. S. A.), born 1820, died 1888; married, first, Lucy T. Jones (b. 1820, d. 1855), and, second, Indiana W. Baytop (b. 1832).

 (c) Lucy Lee (b. 1824), married Capt. Americus V. Wiatt, and died on the Pacific ocean s. p.

 For descendants of the above see Montague Genealogy, 1621-1894, by Geo. W. Montague.

II. Elizabeth, born March 8th, 1757, died s. p.

III. John Segar (b. August 8th, 1753, d. October 21st, 1821);
married three times: first, Catherine Tomkies (June, 1784),
daughter of Col. Francis and Elizabeth (Cooke) Tomkies;
issue:

(1) Jane, born April 14th, 1785, died August, 1790.

(2) Robert, born June 14th, 1787, died August, 1788.

(3) John Segar, born March 4th, 1789, died March 15th,
1847 s. p., and left his property to his cousin, Albert G.
Stubbs of Richmond, Va.

(4) Francis Tomkies, born December 13th, 1791, died
April 22d, 1828, s. p.

Married, *second,* Hannah Montague (b. 1752), widow
Thacker Campbell, with one son, James Campbell. Issue:

(5) Louisa Campbell, married, 1821, Dr. William Graham
Wiatt (Sheriff Gloucester county 1831), and had issue:

(a) Rev. William E. (b. July 31st, 1826), Baptist, chaplain C. S. A.; married three times: first, Bettie Spencer
of King and Queen county; issue:

(*a*) William, married, and living in Kansas; married,
second, Lottie Coleman of Alabama; issue:

(*b*) Addison, married Isabel Slingerland, and lives in
Minneapolis, Minn., and has Lottie and Ed. Slingerland.

(*c*) John, professor in Agricultural and Mechanical College, Auburn, Ala.; married Bettie Wright of Norfolk county, Virginia.

(*d*) Laura, married George Field, the present sheriff of
Gloucester county, Virginia; issue: (1) William
Wiatt, (2) William Stephen, (3) Clara Walker, (4)
Charlotte Laura, (5) John Addison, (6) George
Booth, (7) Mary Lee, (8) Catesby Todd, (9) Ed.
Graham, (10) Lucy Jones, (11) Fred Walker.

(*e*) Mary Lee, married Mac Tinsley (s. p.)

Married, third, Nannie Haywood; issue:

(*f*) Nannie, married ———.

(*g*) Leila, married John Brockenborough.

(*h*) Robert.

(*i*) Mary.

(b) Capt. Americus Vespucius, married, first, Lucy Lee
Montague, who died on a voyage in the Pacific Ocean
(s. p.); second, Alice Jones, issue, Lucy, married
Reynolds of Norfolk, Va.

(c) Alexander Taliaferro (C. S. A.), Clerk of Gloucester

county, Va., married Maud Sinclair, daughter Robert
M. and Rowena (Baytop) Sinclair; issue: (*a*) Mary
Rowena, (*b*) Robert Graham, (*c*) Maud Sinclair, (*d*)
Eleanor Baytop, (*e*) Fay (*f*) Alex. Todd, (*g*) Hawte,
(*h*) Jack, (*i*) Helen, (*k*) Margarete (*l*) Herbert, (*m*)
Americus Vespucius.

(6) Catherine, married, first, Benjamin Hackney of King
and Queen county; second, Capt. George Hoskins issue:

(a) Dr. William Dunbar Hoskins, of King and Queen
county, Virginia, married Janette Carter Roy; issue:

   (*a*) Lucy Bird, married Robert Samuel Dudley; issue, Douglas and Janette.

   (*b*) William Dunbar, married Ellie Hundley; issue
(1) Gladys, (2) John Hundley, (3) Ella Garnett,
(4) Willard.

   (*c*) Betsy Lyne, married Hon. Andrew Jackson Mon-
tague, formerly Attorney General and now (1902)
Governor of Virginia; issue: (1) Matilda Gay, (2)
Janette, (3) Robert Latane.

   (*d*) Charles Roy, married Mattie Liester of Fincastle,
Va.; issue: Janette and another daughter.

   (*e*) Blanche (twin to Matilda), married Hon. John R.
Saunders of Middlesex, Va.; issue, William Alexander.

   (*f*) Matilda (twin to Blanche), married Thomas A.
Henley (s. p.)

   (*g*) Dr. William, of Newport News, Va.

   (*h*) Dr. Robert Roy.

   (*i*) Horace Faulkner.

   (*k*) Juliet, married Leon D. Hicks of South Carolina;
issue: (1) Leon, (2) Judith, (3) William Hoskins.

JOHN SEGAR STUBBS, married, third, Widow Emanuel Macon
Jones of Woodstock, *nee* Isabella C. Fox; issue:

(7) Herbert, who in 1835 sold property in Virginia, moved
to Stewart or Randolph county, Georgia. Descendants,
if any, unknown.

John Segar Stubbs was a man of affairs; was Sheriff of Gloucester county, Va., in 1787-89; emancipated his slaves in 1821;
was Captain in Revolution, and received 4,000 acres of land for
services. He sold "Mulberry Hall" to Stephen Field in 1796.

IV. Francis Smith, (b. December 27th, 1755, d. 1820), married, by Rev. Thos. Hughes, 21st October, 1793, Sarah
Jane, daughter of Charles Tomkies; issue:

(1) Jane Segar, born March 4th, 1796, died 1824; married William B. Hughes; no issue.

(2) Charles Tomkies, born 14th September, 1798, died young.

(3) Dr. Randolph Smith, born September 3d, 1800, died s. p.

(4) Edward Allen, born September 30th, 1802, died s. p.

(5) Rev. Robert Francis, born November 11th, 1805, died 1868; married, first, Jane Chapman, no issue; second, Susan Gaines, issue, Robert Francis (b. 1859, d. 1883, s. p.)

(6) Albert Gallatin, a famous teacher, born February 24th, 1809, died May 8th, 1865; married Elizabeth Coulling; issue

   (a) Mary Lizzie, born May 4th, 1840, died June 8th, 1865, s. p.

   (b) Sarah Jane, of Richmond, Va., born July 10th, 1842; married, 1868) E. P. Hudgins (d. March 23d, 1902) of Mathews county, Va.; issue:

     (1) Albert Perrin, born July 17th, 1869, died August 8th, 1870.

     (2) Mary Ellen, born August 23rd, 1870; married Oscar Hudgins and has issue, (a) Edith Duval, (b) Emma Katherine, (c) Archibald Perrin.

     (3) Elizabeth, born February 5th, 1873.

     (4) Julia Sledd, born January 5th, 1875.

     (5) Gilbert Lee, born March 5th, 1877.

     (6) Alice Belle, born July 26th, 1879, died October 23d, 1883.

     (7) John Douglass, born June 30th, 1883.

   (c) Ellen Douglass, born June 22d, 1845.

   (d) Robert Francis, born November 30th, 1847, died June 21st, 1848.

   (e) Harriet Alberta, born May 30th, 1849, died June 9th, 1869.

   (f) James Coulling, born March 17th, 1851, died August 31st, 1858.

Mrs. Sarah Jane Stubbs, married, second, Ed. Garrett of King and Queen county. No issue.

Francis S. Stubbs was Deputy Sheriff of Gloucester county, Va., a soldier in the Revolution, and received for services 100 acres of land. He lived and died on North River, in Gloucester county, Va.

V. Jane, daughter of John and Jane Stubbs, born June 6th, 1758, died young.

VI. Robert, son of John and Jane Stubbs, born February 13th, 1761, died young.

(B) FRANCIS, son of Capt. John and Mildred (Smith) Stubbs, was born February 21st, 1724. He appears as Processioner in vestry book of Petsworth in 1759, and there was on the Commissioners of Revenue books in 1782, "Estate of Francis Stubbs, 536 acres." Nothing further is known of him.

(C) ELIZABETH, daughter of Capt. John and Mildred (Smith) Stubbs, born January 28th, 1726. Nothing known of her.

(D) PETER, son of Capt. John and Mildred (Smith) Stubbs, born February 12th, 1728, living in 1789, as his name occurs in an old survey; married ——, and had issue:
  I. Lieut. John of the Navy in the Revolution, never married. Land warrants for his services issued to John Bespritch, and Elizabeth Beveridge, Read Purcell and James Purcell, only heirs of John Stubbs.
  II. Frances, married John Bespritch, and had:
    (1) John, married Mrs. Rosanna Shackelford, *nee* Stubbs; no issue.
    (2) Elizabeth, married William Beveridge, and had William, of Baltimore, Md.
  III. Martha, married Nelson Purcell, and had:
    (1) Johannah, born March 28th, 1787, died young.
    (2) Peter, born February 20th, 1790, died young.
    (3) Thomas Nelson, born April 13th, 1792, died young.
    (4) William Reade, born September 1st, 1785, died April 22d, 1848; married Charity Massey (d. December, 1849) and had issue:
    (a) Richard Washington, born May 11th, 1812, died young.
    (b) William Nelson, born March 20th, 1816; married Miss Blake and had:
    (*a*) Mann, born 1845, died in Confederate States Army (s. p.)
    (*b*) William, born 1847, married Margaret Walden; issue, Agnes, Ada and Nelson.
    (*c*) Alexander, born 1849, died 1884 (s. p.)
    (*d*) Alfred, born 1854.
    (*e*) Thomas, born 1858.

(c) Horace Allen, died June 1st, 1888; married, October 31st, 1845, Ann M. Griffin (d. 1900). He resided until death on the place of his grandfather, Peter Stubbs. Issue:

    (*a*) Thomas Reade, born August 24th, 1868; married, 1890, Florence Banks; issue: (1) Amy L., (2) Grover Newbold, (3) Annie L. Jones. He still lives on the old place of his ancestor, Peter Stubbs.

    (*b*) Virgy, born 1881.

    (*c*) Anne Ruth, born 1884.

    (*d*) Marion, born 1877.

    (*e*) Lloyd, born 1870, died 1894.

    (*f*) Horace, died 1899.

(d) Martha Ann, married Caleb M. Fletcher (b. 1825). Issue:

    (*a*) Willie.

    (*b*) Mary, married George H. Enos, and has Mary, Kate and Cassius.

    (*c*) Theodosia, married Richard Bridges; issue, Carrie and Linwood.

(e) Mary Stubbs, born January 14th, 1810, died 1889; married Thaddeus Moore. No issue.

(5) James, married Elizabeth Oakes (d. 1846). Descendants not known to writer.

(E) THOMAS STUBBS, son of Capt. John and Mildred (Smith) Stubbs, born 1733, died before 1794. Lived at Cappahosic in 1776. Advertises, in 1780, that he will leave the colony. Is believed to be the father of John Stubbs, "Younger," who sold Cappahosic tract in 1786 to Stephen Field; and who married, about 1780, Margaret, daughter of William (Sr.) and Elizabeth (Holden) Taliaferro.* Issue:

---

*In the old Chancery papers of Williamsburg, Virginia, is found a suit, from which the following is taken: George Holden, a son of George (student at William and Mary College, 1763), of Ware parish, Gloucester county, Va. Will, 2d January, 1777. (Witness, Mrs. Mary Mason Booth.) Leaves widow (*nee* Susannah Perrin) who marries (II.) Samuel Washington (d. 1795), and two daughters: (1) Ann, died in infancy; (2) Susannah, who marries Nath. Burwell. Susannah, dying before 1795, twenty years old, left one child, who died an infant. Burwell claimed lands as tenant by courtesy and personal property in fee. In this will of George Holden mention is made of his sister, Elizabeth Holden (dead before 1803), wife of William Taliaferro, Sr., of King and Queen county, and her children as follows: Ann, died young; William Taliaferro, Jr.; Margaret Taliaferro, dead before 1803, married (before 1795) John Stubbs, deceased, with infants Margaret Holden and Martha

(1) Margaret Holden, married *circa,* 1803, Richard Taliaferro, second wife; first wife, Miss Wedderburn; issue:

(a) John P., of Toddsbury, married Eleanor Anderson; issue:

(a) John Albert, of Gloucester Point, born 1853, married Mary Lou (d. 1900), daughter M. Boswell and Sallie (Burke) Seawell, and has a son, Philip Boswell (b. 1890).

(b) Hansford Edward, of Zanoni, born 1855, married Fannie, daughter Major William K. and Lucy (Jones) Perrin; issue: (1) William Perrin (b. 1892), (2) Eleanor Anderson (b. 1894), (3) Mollie Wellford (b. 1899).

(c) Richard, of "Hockley," Gloucester county, Virginia, married Widow Samuel Powell Bird, *nee* Fannie Johnson, of Baltimore, Md., and has Earl (b. 1896).

(d) Willie Hockley, born 1860, married Pearline Lucile Kent of Harrisburg, Va.; issue, Kent.

(e) Eleanor.

(f) Bernard Anderson, born 1866.

(2) Martha Haines, married, August 20th, 1805, William Robinson; issue:

(a) William, married Octavia Jennings of Baltimore, Md.; issue:

(a) Alice, married Ed. Valentine, the sculptor, of Richmond, Va.

(b) Octavia.

(c) William, Professor in a college in Maryland, married and has issue.

(d) Needler J.

(b) Benjamin, married Lucy H. Moore of "Chelsea," King William county, Va.; issue:

(a) Lizzie, married Dr. Jno. D. Turner of Richmond; issue: Penn, married; (2) Nannie; (3) Louisa (d), married J. N. Jones, and had Edith; (4) Eddy, married; (5) Benjamin; (6) Mary; (7) William; (8) Lucy; (9) Robert.

(b) Lieper, of Richmond, Va., married Miss Mary S. Campbell, daughter of Charles Campbell, the histo-

---

Haines Stubbs; and Eliza Taliaferro, married John Wedderburn, and fifth child, Mary, married (1793) John Keith and dead before 1795. Nat. Burwell married (II.), 1798, Ann Rich Willis, daughter of Francis and Eliza (Carter) Willis of Whitehall, Gloucester county, Va.

rian.  Issue:  (1)  Russell;  (2)  Lieper M.

(*c*)  Benjamin, married Miss Elizabeth Taylor and had Benjamin, James and Kate.

(*d*)  Nannie.

(*e*)  Mary Prosser, dead.

(*f*)  Kate, dead.

(F)  WILLIAM, son of Capt. John and Mildred (Smith) Stubbs, born 1735, died 1778; married Elizabeth New (d. 1778), sister of Anthony New (b. 1747, d. 1833 in Kentucky), M. C. from Virginia and Kentucky.  Issue:

I.  Francis, born 1764, died 1820; married Elizabeth Dudley and lived at "Stubbs," now Belle Roi; issue:

(1)  Maria Frances, married Simon Stubblefield; no issue.

(2)  Elizabeth New, married George Enos; issue:

(a)  Martha, married James Croswell; no issue.

(b)  Lewis, married Miss Puller, daughter Stephen Puller; issue: (*a*) Julia, married William (Buck) Haywood, and had James K., C. S. A. (d. 1870), who married Miss Hawkins, and had Wilmer (died), married Lucinda Pointer—and had a daughter.

(3)  Rosina, married John Shackelford; issue, Zach, married and has children living in Portsmouth, Va.

(4)  Mary Frances, died young.

II.  James New, of "Valley Front," born 1769, died February 14th, 1814; married, 1797, Rebecca Robins (b. April 21st, 1780, d. October 9th, 1843), daughter of William and Dorothy (Boswell) Robins of Level Green.  (See Robins excursus.)

(1)  Elizabeth New, born July 16th, 1798, died October 16th, 1799.

(2)  James Robins, born October 17th, 1800, died February 22d, 1827; member of the firm of Cole, Shelton & Stubbs of Williamsburg and Gloucester county, Va.; married, May 19th, 1825, Martha Maria Robins (d. January, 1827) ; see Robins excursus; no issue.

(3)  Mary Ann New, born March 6th, 1803, died September 18th, 1823; married, September 11th, 1823, Henry Hughes.  No issue.

(4)  William Francis, born January 1st, 1805, died September 17th, 1824,

(5)  Martha Reade, born Sept. 19th, 1807, died October 23d, 1813.

(6)  John Baytop, born July 22d, 1809, died October, 1812.

(7)  Alexander Day, born September 4th, 1813, died June, 1814.

(8) Jefferson W., of "Valley Front," born March 30th, 1811, died January 22d, 1897; Presiding Justice of Gloucester county, President Gloucester Charity School, Recording Steward of M. E. Church, South; married, March 4th, 1835, Ann Walker Carter, daughter of Capt. James and Lucy Taliaferro (Catlett) Baytop of Springfield; issue:

(a) Rebecca Robins, died young, Sept. 2nd, 1850.

(b) Lucy Ellen, died December 24th, 1877, a dutiful daughter, a devoted sister, a noble woman.

(c) Major James New, C. S. A., lawyer, State Senator, of "Churchill," Gloucester county, Va.; married Eliza, daughter of Joseph and Hester (Shackelford) Medlicott; issue:

(*a*) Jefferson Dunbar, graduate Louisiana State University, now a farmer in Gloucester county; married Edna Coleman (d. January 4th, 1896); issue, Rebecca Robins.

(*b* William Carter, a farmer in Gloucester county.

(*c*) Emma Linwood.

(*d*) John Catlett, died October 14th, 1879.

(*e*) Samuel Medlicott, of Philadelphia.

(*f*) James Lucien, Norfolk, Va.

(d) Thomas Jefferson, A. M., Ph. D. (C. S. A.), Professor William and Mary College; married Mary Mercer, daughter of Capt. Joseph B. and Louisa Mercer (Waller) Cosnahan, of Williamsburg, Va.; issue:

(*a*) Mary Louisa, died November 10th, 1870.

(*b*) Ann Waller Carter.

(*c*) Robert Catlett, died August 13th, 1876.

(*d*) Jefferson Lawrence, died March 2d, 1879.

(*e*) Thomas Jefferson, Jr., A. M. of William and Mary College, now a student of Johns Hopkins University.

(*f*) Lucy Taliaferro.

(*g*) Mary Mercer.

(e) Wm. Carter, Ph. D. (C. S. A.), Director State Experiment Stations of Louisiana; married Elizabeth Saunders Blair, daughter of Henry D. and Mary Louisa (Saunders) Blair. No issue.

(f) Mary Ann, died 1893.

(g) Dr. John Catlett, of Baltimore, died 1874, s. p. Educated at University of Virginia and graduated in medicine at University of Maryland, and a promising young physician in Baltimore at time of his death; a

boy of spotless character and a man without **reproach.**
(h) Martha Maria, now mistress of "Valley Front."
(i) Elizabeth Baytop, of "Valley Front."
(j) Francis Dunbar, died young.
(k) Susannah Robins, died young.
III. Ann (b. *circa* 1763), married (second wife) Richard
Coleman (b. January 18, 1761), a soldier of the Revolution, member of Capt. Nath. Welch's Company, Second
Virginia Regiment, Col. William Brent, and was honorably discharged in 1780. Issue:
(1) Claiborne, married Johanna Hall; issue:
   (a) John William, married Miss Tomlinson; issue:
      (*a*) Warner.
      (*b*) William.
      (*c*) Ida, married Browne.
      (*d*) Johanna, married Plack.
   (b) Dr. Warner W., graduate Jefferson College, Phila-
      delphia, married Miss Wismer of Philadelphia, and
      had issue: Claudius, married —— of Ashland, Va.,
      and has issue: (1) Cora, married ——; (2) Emmett;
      (3) Alvin.
   (c) Matilda, married Thomas Simcoe (d.); issue:
      (*a*) Doctor, married Alice Eastwood; no issue.
      (*b*) Henry C., killed in C S. A., s. p.
   (d) Catherine, married John F. Kemp (d.); issue:
      (*a*) John Thomas, married Miss Whitfield; issue,
      John.
      (*b*) Maggie, married Thomas Pagaud; issue: (A)
      Maggie, married John Miller, issue John and Lin-
      wood; (B) Thomas, married ——, issue Thomas;
      (C) Eulalie, married Thomas Hansford, no issue;
      (D) Ida, married Elmer Davis, issue one child;
      (E) Etta, married Wilmer Crocket, issue Lettie;
      (F) Linwood; (G) Lucy.
      (*c*) Lucy, married Samuel Dennis; issue, Eddie
      Byron.
      (*d*) Cordelia, married, first, John Enos; issue: (A)
      Annie, married St. Clair, issue Jack; (B) Ocie,
      married ——; married, second, Burchett; no is-
      sue.
   (e) Emily, d., s. p.
   (f) Laudiskie, married W. E. Howell; issue:
      (*a*) Gertrude, married J. H. Holmes.
      (*b*) Perrin.
      (*c*) Harold.

(g) Aurelius, married Miss Tremmer; issue: (A) Lettie, (B) Annie, (C) Avis, (D) Arthur.

(h) Ocie, married W. T. Drewry; issue: (A) William, (B) Estelle (C) Eula.

(2) Carter, married Widow Collier *nee* Puller (d.) ; issue:

(a) Rebecca (d.), married Thomas Blake; issue: Stephen Decatur, and perhaps others.

(b) James, married Emily Williams.

(3) Richard, married Miss Hall; issue: Lucy (d.), married John Moore, issue Richard, killed C. S. A.

(4) Thomas, married Harriet Stubbs (d.) ; issue:

(a) John F., married Mildred Brock Philpotts; issue:

(*a*) Martha Jane, married Benjamin C. Newcomb; issue: (1) Malvern, married Bertha Stubbs; (2) Clara O'Neal (d. 1900), married Dr. F. F. Davis, no issue; (3) Lloyd (student at University of Virginia) ; (4) Coleman; (5) Martha; (6) William (student at William and Mary College; (7) Oakley.

(*b*) Frank, married Eliza Holland; no issue.

(*c*) Hettie (d.), married Julius Roane (d.) ; issue: (1) William, (2) John, (3) Frank.

(*d*) Mildred, married William Simpson; issue, Lena.

(*e*) Margaret, married Peter Turney; no issue.

(*f*) Albert Thomas, married, first, Mary Lou Gaskins, no issue; second, Louisa Teague South, no issue.

(*g*) John Currin, died young.

(b) Martha Robins, married, first, William Caffee; issue:

(a) Mary (d.), married John H. Flood (d.), of Lynchburg, Va.; issue: (1) Thomas, (2) Bessie, (3) Heber, (4) French, (5) Grace, (6) Nellie, (7) William.

(b) Bettie married Moseley of Buckingham county, Va.; issue: (1) Fannie; (2) Mattie; (3) Jane, married Rev. Henderlite.

Married, second, John N. Sale; issue:

(c) William J., of Roanoke, Va., married, first, Sue Chapman of Montgomery, Va.; issue (1) Stewart O., married Mattie O'Neal Fudge of Marion, Va.; (2) John Bowman, married Fannie Weaver of Norfolk, Va.; (3) Mattie, married Stephenson of Smyth county, Va.; (4) Nannie, married Davis of Max Meadows, Va.; (5) Marvin, married Myrtle

Weaver, of Norfolk, Va.; (6) Daisy.

Married, *second,* Mary Scott, of Marion, Va.; issue: (7) William Roy.

(d) Lucy O'Neal, married Granville H. Fudge of Marion, Va.; issue:' Martha O'Neal, married Stewart O. Sale.

(e) A. Jefferson, married Bettie Wilson, of Lynchburg, Va.; issue: (A) Daniel, (B) Grace, (C) Willie, (D) Graham.

(c) Randall, married ——; issue, Julia.

(d) Jane Amy, married Ed. S. Stubbs; issue:

(a) Andrew, married Cordelia Stubbs; issue: (1) Edgar Smith, (2) Mary Amy.

(b) Ed. S., married Mary Ella Smith; issue: (1) Clarence; (2) Lena, (3) Edith), (4) Edward, (5) Herbert; (6) Eloise; (7) Catherine; (8) Ruth.

(c) Octavia, married William Henry Curry (d. 1902), C. S. A.; issue: (1) William Shield, (2) Charles Sowersby, Married Ida May Henderson; (3) George Washington; (4) Walter Clifton; (5) Ada Jane.

(d) Hettie, married George D. Stubbs; issue: (1) Bertha (b. 1880), married (1898) Malvern Newcomb; (2) Marvin (b. 1882); (3) Landon Ellwood (b. 1888).

(e) Richard Claiborne, married, first, Elizabeth Sale; married, second, Susan Pointer, widow Joseph H. Wiatt (no issue). Issue by first wife: Rosa, married Gayle and has issue: (1) Lilian, married and has issue: (2) Byron, married and has issue.

(f) Elizabeth Ann, married Capt. Augustus Williams; issue:

(a) Elizabeth, married C. A. Shafer; issue: (1) Adam; (2) Woolsey, married Miss Marshall of Berkeley, Va.; (3) Mary Elizabeth, married, first, Henry Culpeper of Portsmouth, Va., and has issue; married, second, Boone, no issue; (4) Claiborne, killed in C. S. A.; (5) Emily, married James Coleman, no issue.

(5) James, married, first, Mildred Wright; issue:

(a) Nannie Stubbs, married Capt. H. Thornton Philpotts of Norfolk, Va.; issue:

(a) Willie C. (d., s. p.)

(b) Eudora Quigg (d.), married Geo. E. Croswell; issue: (A) William Edward; (B) Nannie Pearl, married Richard Lambert, issue, Allen; (C) Oakley; (D) Margaret Etta, married Harry Guy of Norfolk, Va.

(c) James Thornton, married Emma Ashby; issue, Mary Linda.

Married, second, Mary Medlicott; issue:

(b) Capt. Richard Cole, of "The Island," Gloucester county, Virginia; married Isabella Anderson (d.), of Clarksville, Va.; issue:

(a) Willie Clifford, died young.

(b) Minnie Cole, married Robert E. Wilson (d. 1902), no issue.

(c) Edna Elizabeth (d. 1896), married Jeff D. Stubbs; issue, Rebecca Robins.

(d) Nannie Bell, married J. Presley Williams; issue: (1) Richard; (2) Isabel Norman; (3) Ethel Lee.

(e) Olivia Norman.

(f) Ethel Lee.

(g) Alice Bland.

(h) Maud Arendale.

(i) Mary Anderson.

(c) Mary Elizabeth, married Robert B. Wilson; no issue.

(6) William, married ——, and had issue: Mildred, married Thruston.

(7) Elizabeth, married John Wilson; issue:

(a) Sarah Ann, married Jasper C. Hughes; issue: (a) Julia, married, *first,* John W. Leigh, C. S. A.; issue: (1) Lizzie, married Heber Moore and has issue; (2) Julian, married ——; (3) William, married Ella Philpotts; issue, Claude, Lucy, Linda, Fannie, Rosa, Julia and Willie; married, *second,* R. Overton Allard; issue, (4) Roswell, married.

(8) Louisa, married Billy Lawson; no issue.

*Descendants of Lawrence, the Son of John and Mildred (Smith) Stubbs.*

LAWRENCE, born 1738, died October 26th, 1797; married (1763) Ellis Duval, born 1738, died February 4th, 1798; issue:

(I.) FRANCIS, born May 1st, 1773, died January 12th, 1805; married, first, Susannah Robins; issue:

(a) William Robins (b. 1799, d. January 10th, 1880), Justice, Steward of M. E. Church, South, a man of highest integrity; married, first, Mary Cole Stubbs; second, Mary Jane Stubbs; no issue.

William Robins emancipated his slaves.

Second wife, Nancy Hall; issue:

(b) Catherine, married Thomas Wright and moved to Indiana, and has five children.

(II.) LAWRENCE SMITH (born March 1st, 1778, died June 17th, 1828), of "Providence," Gloucester county, Va.; married, July 12th, 1801, Mary Ann Davis; issue:

(a) Elizabeth, born 1803, died young.

(b) Mary Ann, born March 2d, 1805, died January 7th, 1874; married, June 26th, 1822, Sowersby Curry; issue:

(a) Martha Ann Curry (b. 1830), married Henry A. Howard (b. 1801, d. 1863), C. S. A.; issue:

(1) Alice A. (b. 1850), married John Wesley Gregg; issue: Mary Ann, married Richard Sterling, no issue.

(2) Emma Jane (b. 1852), married Thomas Leigh; issue: 1, Willetta, b. 1874; 2, Thomas E., b. 1876; 3, Verna Belle, b. 1878; 4, Cordelia A., b. 1882; 5, Richard Henry, b. 1886; 6, Susannah M., b. 1890; 7, Alice Anna E., b. 1893; 8, James M., b. 1896.

(3) Susie A. (b. 1854), married John W. Blake of Baltimore; issue: 1, Howard, married; 2, Mattie; 3, Emma; 4, Louis; 5, Carroll.

(4) William Lee (b. 1856), married Fannie Rowe, daughter William Rowe; issue: 1, Ernest Linwood, b. 1885; 2, Bettie Lee, b. 1887; 3, Emma Virginia, b. 1890; 4, Maria America, b. 1893; 5, Thomas Lawrence, b. 1897.

(5) Henry A. (b. 1860), married Eugenia Leigh, daughter of Dr. J. H. S. and ——— (Harwood) Leigh; issue: 1, Henry Allen; 2, Mattie Virginia.

(b) America Curry (b. 1838, d. 1882), married P. Mack Brooke, C. S. A.; issue:

(1) Ella, married Carpenter, and has several children.

(2) Anna, married Charley Dobson, son of Joseph Dobson; issue: (1) Ernest, (2) ———, (3) Maude.

(3) Willie.

(4) Emma, married Sam Harris; issue: 1, Oliver.

(c) Maria H. Curry (d. February, 1901), married

(c) Maria H. Curry (d. February, 1901), married Thomas E. Freeman (Co. D, 24th Virginia Cavalry); issue:

(1) Eddie, married Mrs. Griffith; no issue.

(2) Benjamin.

(3) William Henry, married Fannie ———; issue: 1, William; 2, Eva; 3, Marion.

(4) Maryus.

(5) Jane, married ——.
(*d*) William Henry Curry (b. 1837, d. 1902), married, first, Martha Ann Stubbs, no issue; second, Octavia Stubbs; issue:
   (1) William Henry Shields.
   (2) Charles Sowersby, married Ida May Henderson; issue: 1, Burwell Garnett.
   (3) George Worthington.
   (4) Clifton.
   (5) Ada Jane.
(c) Martha Ann Smith, born October 12th, 1809, died August 4th, 1843; married (first wife) Dr. Daniel D. Hall, and moved to Connersville, Fayette county, Ind.; issue:
   (*a*) James Lawrence, born 1829, died young.
   (*b*) Priscilla Ann (b. 1831, d.), married Dr. Scaife Whiting Hughes (d.); issue: Ella S., married C. E. J. McFarland, of Connersville, Ind.
   (*c*) Mary Susan, born 1834, unmarried.
   (*d*) Alfred Stubbs, born in Gloucester county, Va., married —— (d. '96), and now lives at 923 Eighteenth avenue, Seattle, Wn.; no issue.
   (*e*) Martha Elizabeth (b. 1838), married Dr. J. D. Latimore of Shidler, Delaware county, Ind.
(d) William Francis of "Old Ark" (b. May 23d, 1812, d. July 21st, 1847), married, March 4th, 1835, Mary Jane Stubbs (d. 1899); issue
   (*a*) Ann Maria Smith, born January 20th, 1837, died 1872 (s. p.)
   (*b*) William Robb, born 1839, died young.
   (*c*) James Lawrence (b. September 13th, 1841, d. 1899), C. S. A., unmarried; a superb soldier and excellent citizen.
   (*d*) Mary Catherine, born September 4th, 1844, died 1893; unmarried.
(e) Lawrence Smith (b. April 4th, 1818, d. December 18th, 1891), married, July 24th, 1839, Mary Dame; issue:
   (*a*) Martha Ann (b. July 27th, 1840, d. March 26th, 1880), married William Henry Curry (first wife), no issue.
   (*b*) Mary Frances (b. January 10th, 1842, d.), married, 1868, Isom Martin Leavitt (d), C. S. A.; issue:
      (1) Florina, married, first, John Bohannon; issue: 1, Jessie, died young; 2, George. Married, second, —— Morgan; issue, two children.

(2) Mary, married Edgar Smith of Portsmouth; issue, Lydia.

(3) Emmett Martin, married Carrie ——, and has three children.

(4) Lawrence.

(5) Martin.

(6) Lelia, married Wilkie Barnes; issue, Lelia Goldye, b. 1901.

(7) Linwood.

(*c*) Lawrence Smith (b. 23d January, 1844, d. 1877), C. S. A., married, August 11th, 1870, Agnes Hall; issue:

(1) Norman Elmo, of Baltimore, Md.

(2) Maud.

(*d*) Cordelia (b. May 20th, 1847, d. March 16th, 1886), married, Dec. 25th, 1872, Andrew Stubbs. (For issue see page 38.)

(*e*) George Daniel (b. November 20th, 1852), merchant of Belle Roi, married, December 25th, 1877, Hettie Roselia Stubbs. (For issue see page 38.)

(*f*) Walter E. (b. June 6th, 1960), married Annie Brooks; issue:

(1) Walter, born 1884.

(2) Carlisle, born 1889.

(III.) John Smith of King and Queen county (b. 1786, d. 1820), married (1814) first, Mary Baytop; no issue. Married, second, Mary Roy Chapman; issue:

(a) Mary Jane (b. 1817, d. 1900), married William Francis Stubbs. (For issue see page 41.)

(b) William Wiley, married, first, Lucy Eastwood and had:

(*a*) Fannie, married William Hughes; issue:

(1) William Stubbs.

Married, second, Mary Eastwood; issue:

(*b*) William Robins, married Mrs. Octavia Bland, *nee* Anderson; no issue.

(*c*) Mary Sue, married Octavius J. Harcum; issue: (1) Octavius Marvin, (2) Marius, (3) Roy.

(*d*) Marion, married Ann Trevellian; issue: (1) Lloyd, (2) Mary, (3) Doswell.

(c) John Lawrence, married Lucy Ann Meacham; no issue. She married, second, William Duval Stubbs; no issue.

(IV.) William Duval Stubbs, of Fiddler's Green (b. Feb-

ruary 25th, 1771, d. July 28th, 1840), married, first
(September 8th, 1798), Polly Graves (d. 1822) ; issue:
(a) Ann (b. June 27th, 1799, d. 1822), married, 1820, John
Martin, and had issue:
(*a*) John, married Emma Shackelford, and had issue:
(1) Annie, married Samuel Bowman of Richmond;
issue: 1, Marvin; 2, Lillian.
(2) Alice, unmarried.
(3) Emma, married William H. Clements, C. S. A.,
of Richmond; issue: Harvey (b. 1871, d. 1900),
married Jennie Otey; issue: 1, Allen; 2, Virginia.
(b) Maria Duval (b. Sept. 24th, 1805), married, 1824
(second wife), John Martin; issue:
(*b*) Alexander Hersey (d. 1884), Sheriff Gloucester
county, married, first, Hester Mitchell, no issue; married, second, Louisa Medlicott; issue:
(1) Paul (b. 1869), of Norfolk, Va.
(*c*) Matilda C. (b. 1824, d. 1900), unmarried.
(*d*) Mary Ann (b. 1831, d. 1884), married Alexander
Shackelford, C. S. A. (d. 1902) ; issue:
(1) Nora, married Rev. T. J. Wray of Virginia, M.
E. Church, South; no issue.
(2) Mary Lester, married Maris V. Kerns; issue:
1, Martin; 2, Vernon; 3, Mary Ann.
(*e*) Martha (b. 1833, d. 1857), married (first wife) Geo.
E. Shackleford; who married, *second*, Ellen Medlicott. Issue by first wife:
(1) Benjamin (b. 1854), married Lula Joiner; issue:
(1) Hugh, (2) Hazel.
(2) Carrie (b. 1856), married Sam'l Wyatt Tinsley;
issue: (1) Woodland, (2) Morgan.
(*f*) Wm. Henry (b. 1835, d. 1890), Captain on Gen. T.
L. Rosser's staff, C. S. A., married, first, Mildred
Kemp (d. 1874) ; issue:
(1) Johnnie (d.), married Columbia Lambeth; issue:
1, Fred; 2, Mary; 3, Annie; 4, a boy.
(2) Mattie, married Johnny Butler; no issue.
(3) Wm. H.
(4) James, married Otelia Bland, and has issue.
(5) Philip.
Wm. Henry married, second, Adeline Leigh; no issue.
John Martin married, third, Miss Duval, and had:
(*g*) Philip, married Indiana Medlicott.
(c) Mary Cole (b. Nov. 23d, 1803, d. 1868)), married
Wm. Robins Stubbs; no issue.

(d) John (b. Nov. 17th, 1801, d. ——), married, first, Sallie Stevens; issue:

(*a*) Wm. Duval, married Mrs. Jno. Lawrence Stubbs, *nee* Virginia Meachum; no issue.

(*b*) Mary Ann, died s. p.

(*c*) Jno. Stevens, married Mrs. Ladd of Richmond, **Va.** Issue: (1) Jno. W. Secretary Y. M. C. A. in Portsmouth, and two daughters.

(*d*) Robt., married Ann Richardson; no issue. She married, second, W. P. R. Leigh.

Married, second, Virginia Mitchell; issue:

(*e*) James Monroe (C. S. A.) of Oakley, married, first, Parthenia Didlake; issue: (1) Robert, married ——; (2) John W.; (3) and (4).

Married, second, Alma Roy; issue: one child.

(*f*) Wilbur Fisk, died in 1900 in Baltimore; **married**; issue unknown.

(*g*) Silas, married, and lives at Shady Grove, Hanover county, Va.

(V.) MILDRED SMITH STUBBS, born July 19th, 1765, died October 1th, 1824; married John Mitchel; issue:

(a) William Duval (b. 1795), married Frankie Smither; issue:

(*a*) Albert, married —— Fary, and has issue:
(1) Julius, married.
(2) Warren, married Eva Roane.
(3) Russell.

(*b*) Matilda, married Charles Roane; issue:
(1) Rev. Hamilton, of Baltimore Methodist **Conference**, and has issue.
(2) Elva, married William White of Norfolk, and **has** issue.
(3) Floyd, of Portsmouth, married Emma Shackelford, daughter of William Shackelford, and has two children.
(4) Aubrey.
(5) Minnie.
(6) Linwood (a boy).

(b) John, married —— Curry; no issue.

(c) Frank, married Frances Pointer; issue:

(*a*) William, married —— of Richmond, Va., and has:
(1) Julia, married Turner, a druggist of Richmond.
(2) Lena, (3) A daughter.

(*b*) Virginia, married John Stubbs (see above).

(*c*) Hester, married Alex. Hersey Martin; no issue.

(*d*) Richard, married Miss Mann of Essex, and had:

    (1) Hezekiah G., married Miss Edwards of King George county, Va.; no issue.

    (2) Stubbs, married —— of Essex.

(d) Rev. Alexander Mitchell, of Alabama Methodist Conference; descendants, if any, unknown.

## GEORGIA STUBBSES.

James and Peter Stubbs, believed to be brothers, went to Georgia from Virginia, the one before and the other after the Revolutionary war. They are believed to be the sons of Francis, the son of John and Susannah Stubbs, previously mentioned as living in Gloucester county, Va. It is probable that Benjamin and Allen of the Revolution were either the sons of Francis or Thomas, and that the Thomas of Washington and Wilkinson counties, Ga., given further on, was a son of Benjamin. No descendants of Allen are known.

JAMES STUBBS was in the Georgia line during the Revolution (Smith's Story of Georgia) and is believed to have moved to Georgia circa 1770. He married, circa 1770, Mary Eliza Scott, daughter of Col. James and Frances (Collier) Scott of Prince Edward county, Va., who moved to South Carolina in 1770, and died in 1776. (Scott Family Tree.)

Col. James Scott was son of Col. Thomas Scott, the immigrant who married Ann Baytop, sister of Col. James Baytop, of Springfield, Gloucester county, Virginia, and daughter of Thomas and —— (Alexander) Baytop.

Col. James and Frances (Collier) Scott are the ancestors, also, of the McGehees and Scotts throughout the South.

The issue of James and Mary Eliza (Scott) Stubbs (as far as known) are as follows:

I. ANN, eldest daughter of James and Mary Eliza (Scott) Stubbs (b. 1771), married, 1802, second wife (first wife Miss Scott), Dr. Charles Gachet who escaped in his mother's arms as an infant from the insurrection in San Domingo. His father, returning to his home for some papers after depositing his wife and child safely aboard a vessel, was caught and killed. The mother and child escaped and came to Georgia. Issue:

    (1) Col. JAMES EDWARD (b. 1804, d. 1876), of Chunnennuggie Ridge, Ala., married Lavinia Harrison Jones (b. 1817), who still lives, the pride of a devoted family. Issue:

(a) M. Anne (b. 1836), married, first (1856), Francis L. Deloney (d. 1862), no issue; married, second (1872), Col. John L. Branch, C. S. A. (d. 1894); issue: (a) Annie Lavinia, b. 1874; (b) Edward Gachet, b. 1877.

(b) Capt. Charles (b. 1838), C. S. A., married, 1871, Tallulah Lampkin, d. 1900 (a most beautiful and lovable woman); issue: (a) Dr. James Ed. (b. 1872), married, 1902, Pearle Rivers Malone of Sheffield; (b) Tallulah (b. 1873), married, 1898, Neander M. Woods of Memphis, Tenn; issue, Charles Gachet.

(c) Lucy, married, 1865, Dr. Samuel Pou (d. 1875); issue: (a) Minnie Feldar (b. 1866), married Gus. G. Orr; issue: (1) Gustavus, (2) Samuel; (b) Lucy Gachet (b. 1868), married Charles H. Barnwell; issue, Charles; (c) Lavinia Jones (b. 1873), married Samuel Farnsworth; issue, Jerry and Lutie; (d) Joseph Samuel (b. 1871), married Lucy Cowan, and has issue.

(d) Henry (b. 1844), unmarried.

(e) Molly Lavinia (b. 1849), married, 1875, William H. Smith (b. 1845); issue: (a) Lavinia, b. 1876; (b) Louise, b. 1878; (c) Harry, b. 1880, died young; (d) Gachet, b. 1882; (e) Hogan, b. 1883; (f) Minnie, b. 1885; (g) Lamar, b. 1889; (h) Corinne, b. 1890; (i) Myra, b. 1892.

(f) Nicholas (b. 1854), unmarried.

(2) NICHOLAS, married, first, Janie Jones; issue:

(a) Rochelle, married Mr. Martiniere.

(b) Janie, married Mr. Walls.

(c) James, unmarried.

Married, second, Celia Transum; issue:

(d) Mattie, (e) Lula, (f) Thornwell, (g) William.

(3) CAROLINE, married Henry W. Jernigan; issue:

(a) Dr. Charles, married Cornelia Crawford.

(b) James F., married Belle Tarver.

(c) Frances, married Dr. N. P. Banks of Columbus, Ga.

(4) CHARLOTTE, married Erasmus T. Beale; issue:

(a) Annie, married Pickett.

(b) Epsie, married Mansfield.

(c) Samuel, married Patty Price.

(d) Charlotte, married ——.

II. FRANK (b. 1773), of Eatonton, Putnam county, Ga., married (1795) Miss Booth; issue:

(1) JAMES (b. 1796), died in Putnam county, Georgia; married, first, Lucinda Cotton; issue:

(a) James (b. 1821), married Ellen M. Stubbs (b. 1837);
no issue.
(b) Col. Charles Wesley (b. 1823, d.), C. S. A., married
1849, Eliza W. Stubbs (b. 1832); issue:
(a) Charles Wesely, d. 1875; (b) Thomas Florence;
(c) John W.; (d) Annie Lou (see page 76).
(c) Thomas, unmarried.
Married, second, Martha Sadler; issue:
(d) Joseph R., unmarried.
(2) JOHN or JACK (b. 1798), moved to Copiah county, Miss.,
where he died. Was a patron of races in Natchez, Vicksburg and Memphis. Married Susan Kendrick of Georgia;
issue:
(a) John, b. 1819, d. 1863, at Crystal Springs, Miss.;
married Phœbe Campbell (d. 1878 of yellow fever);
issue: (a) John, died s. p.; (b) Logan, died s. p.
(c) Elwell, married three times, the last time to Mr.
Terry of McComb City, Miss.
(d) Susie, married Mr. Sturges of Crystal Springs,
Miss.
(e) Emma, married Mr. Jones of Crystal Springs, Miss.
(f) Mildred, married Mr. Broomfield of Montgomery,
Texas.
(b) Martha Clements, born at Eatonton, Ga., 1821; married, 1846, Moody Stackhouse of South Carolina (d.
Utica, Miss., in 1894); issue:
(a) Beatrice (b. 1847), married, first (1865), Dr. Henry
C. Stackhouse (d. 1877) of Crystal Springs, Miss.;
issue:
(1) Blanche O. (b. 1866), married, 1885, Charles L.
England of Sparta, Tenn., and lives at Hazlehurst,
Miss.; issue, five children, viz: Beatrice, b. 1886;
Alluzelle, b. 1888; Annie Laurie, b. 1891; Blanche,
b. 1893, and Henry, b. 1898.
(2) Cordelia A. (b. 1870, d. 1899), twin to—
(3) Camilla, d. 1890.
(4) LeGrand Brickell (b. 1873), married (1894)
Mary Mitchell of Hazlehurst, and lives in Crystal
Springs; no issue.
(5) Henri Coma (b. 1877), unmarried.

Beatrice married, second (1883), Hampton England (d. 1886)
of Sparta, Tenn.; no issue. She married, third, W. T. Mathenay, ex-Sheriff of Copiah county, Miss.; no issue.
(b) John Stubbs Stackhouse (b. 1854), married, 1887,

Ellen Coor of Hazlehurst, and lives in Crystal
Springs, Miss.; issue: (1) Camille, b. 1888; (2)
Martha, b. 1890; (3) John, b. 1891; (4) Guy, b.
1893; (5) Lillian, b. 1898.

(c) Frankie Ann (b. 1858), unmarried, and lives in
Utica, Miss.

(c) Ann (b. 1823, d. 1884), married Mr. Broomfield of
Baltimore, Md., and removed to Montgomery, Texas,
and has issue: (a) Jane, died young; (b) Sarah, died
young; (c) Eliza, died young; (d) Louisa, b. 1833, d.
1853; (e) Susan, b. 1834, d. 1853; (f) Mildred, b.
1843, d. 1871, married (1853) A. F. Powell of Willis,
Texas, issue Frank.

(3) PETER (b. 1800), moved to Utica, Miss., where he died;
married, first, Louisa Ward and, second, Sarah Dudley;
issue:

(a) Mary (d. 1868), married James Bolte; issue, Mrs.
Whittaker of Vicksburg, Miss.

(b) Louisa, died in Waco, Texas; married Samuel Cos-
tan; issue, Walter.

(c) Samuel (died 1899), married, first, Julia Kelley; second, Helen Yates; issue: (a) Julia, b. 1880; (b) Nellie,
b. 1888; (c) Houston, b. 1890. All living in Utica,
Miss.

(4) FRANK (b. 1806), never married; lived with his niece,
Miss Martha C. Stackhouse, near Utica, Miss. He ac-
cumulated a large fortune. Committed suicide by stab-
bing, September 17th, 1860. Left his fortune to his
niece and brothers and sisters.

(5) THOMAS BAYTOP, died in Harris county, Ga.; married
a Miss Meadows. Mr. Francis Marion Stubbs of Richardson county, Texas, gives the above information and
says there was also another Thomas Stubbs at the same
time and in the same county, of whom he knew but little.
The other Thomas was evidently the grandfather of Mrs.
Dr. Jenkins, given elsewhere. No descendants of
Thomas and Miss Meadows have been found.

(6) WILLIAM, born 1802, died 1876 in Leake county, Miss.;
married Sarah Duke; issue:

(a) Francis Marion (b. December 22d, 1824), of Richardson, Texas (C. S. A.). He is now old and infirm.
He married first, September 30th, 1849, Mary E. Harris,
and second, August 21st, 1874, Martha L. Trippe. Issue:
by first wife:

(a) Joseph Marion, of Calhoun, Texas (b. January 11th,

1860), married, 1889, Ella Washburn; issue: (1) Marcus Slater, b. 1890; (2) Mary Lou, b. 1892; (3) Flora, b. 1895; (4) Mamie, b. 1900.

(b) Nicholas Harris, of Calhoun, Texas (b. September 3d, 1862), married, January 13th, 1887, Sallie A. Zachary; issue: (1) Charlie Harris, b. 1888; (2) Francis Marion, b. 1891; (3) Flora Azola, b. 1895; (4) Ann Lee, b. 1898.

(c) Charles Peeler (b. December 1st, 1867, d. March 13th, 1896), married, January 22d, 1891, Flora A. Cofer of Frazer, Greer county, Okla.; issue: (1) Ernest Denver, b. 1891; (2) Joseph Marion, b. 1893; (3) Grady Odres, b. 1894; (4) Charles Orion, b. 1896.

(d) Sarah Euphemia (b. June 21st, 1871), married December 28th, 1890, William S. Gray of Town Creek, Lawrence county, Ala. They now live at Allen, Texas. Issue: (1) Florrie Edna, b. 1891; (2) Marion Ruth, b. 1892; (3) Robert Lee, b. 1895.

Issue by second wife:

(e) Julius Hamilton, b. August 5th, 1875.

(f) Robert Lee, of Mot, Bossier parish, La. (b. August 5th, 1878), married, June 21st, 1901, Ludie Dees.

(g) Cornelius Theodore, of Richardson, Texas, born August 21st, 1880.

(h) George Edward, of Richardson, Texas, born March 18th, 1885.

(b) William, born 1830, died 1850 s. p.

(c) Jack J., born 1835, died, 1900, in Plain Dealing, La., where his widow now resides. Lieutenant in Co. C, 16th Alabama Regiment, C. S. A., and a gallant soldier and an excellent school teacher. Married, first (1865), Mrs. Ruth Stein of Stein's Creek, Miss.; issue:

(a) Charles J. (b. October 6th, 1866), married, 1895, Mary Estelle Aills, and has issue, Lizzie, b. 1898.

(b) Mary, now called Sallie, born April 9th, 1868, and is a teacher in Public Schools of Memphis, Tenn; residence 1008 Rayburn avenue.

Married, second (1875), Miss Myles of Texas; issue:

(c) Maggie, b. 1878; (d) George, b. 1879; (e) Ella, b. 1880, died young; (f) Mattie, b. 1881; (g) John, b. 1885.

(d) Charles (b. 1838, d. 1870), C. S. A.; married Jane Wright, who survives him in Arkansas; issue:

(*a*) James (b. November 27th, 1867), of Little Rock, Ark.

(*b*) Frank (b. 1869), of Detroit, Texas.

(e) James W. (b. February 21st, 1839), of Benton, Ark., C. S. A.; married, December 28th, 1869, Mrs. Anne Finch; issue:

(*a*) Willie (b. December 16th, 1870), married, 1895, Mr. D. A. Kent; issue: (1) John, b. 1887; (2) Charlie, b. 1889; (3) Job, b. 1891; (4) James, b. 1893; (5) a daughter, b. 1898.

(*b*) Charlie (b. October 17th, 1872), married, 1901, Tite Miller; no issue.

(*c*) Lizzie (b. December 9th, 1875), married, 1890, Hardie Farmer; issue: (1) James, b. 1891; (2) Pearl, b. 1893; (3) Annie, b. 1896; (4) Dew, died young.

(*d*) Emma, born January 21st, 1878.

(f) Camilla Ann (b. May 13th, 1829), married, 1845, Thomas H. Langford of Alabama; issue:

(*a*) Melissa Ann (b. October 16th, 1846), married, 1866, John Hannah; issue, twelve children.

(*b*) Sarah Elizabeth (b. March 24th, 1848), unmarried.

(*c*) Helen Marina (b. April 30th, 1849), married, 1867, Joseph Reynolds; issue, twelve children.

(*d*) William Henry (b. December 8th, 1850), married Missouri Walls; issue, eight children.

(*e*) Emma Thomas (b. June 2d, 1852, d. 1888), married, 1870, Robert Brittin; issue, seven children.

(*f*) Camilla Eugenia (b. December 11th, 1855), married, first (1877), Thomas Waugh and, second, Jasper Donahoe; issue, seven children.

(*g*) Thomas Patten (b. November 14th, 1858, d. 1898), married, 1894, Anne Franklin; issue, two children.

(*h*) Mary Caroline (b. April 15th, 1861, d. 1896), married, 1883, Robert Waugh; issue, six children.

(*i*) Martha Kendall (b. October 8th, 1864, d. 1902), married, 1889, John Burgess; issue, one child.

(*k*) Thomas H., killed in C. S. A. July 28th, 1864.

(g) Mary Elizabeth (b. October 24th, 1835), married, first (1853), George E. Hydrick (d. 1871) of Charleston, S. C.; married, second (1885), William B. Atkins. Issue by first marriage (none by second):

(*a*) Edward Hydrick (b. December 24th, 1854, d. 1885), married Sallie Tucker; issue: (1) Lewis; (2) Eddie (a girl); (3) Ola; (4) Cora; (5) Aldon (a boy).

(*b*) Charles Morton (b. October 28th, 1859), married Louisa Stokes; issue: (1) George; (2) Roy; (3) Edna; (4) Margaret.

(*c*) Francis Marion (b. January 6th, 1862), married Felicia Cooper; issue: (1) Minnie; (2) Mary; (3) Caroline; (4)Cora; (5) Grover; (6) Alvin; (7) Edward.

(*d*) Mary Adelia (b. April 22d, 1864), married Mr. Mc-Adams; issue: (1) William Curtis; (2) Maud Lee; (3) Isabel; (4) Beulah; (5 and 6, twins) Columbus and Alonzo.

(*e*) George Robert (b. September 22d, 1866), married Adelia McAdams; issue: (1) Alice; (2) Austin; (3) Chapman; (4) Walter; (5) Nellie; (6) Georgia; (7) Bettie.

(*f*) Willie born November 22d, 1869, died, 1901, in Paris, Texas; married Mollie Matthews, who now lives at Stein's Creek, Miss.; issue: (1) Mabelle; (2) Willie; (3) Charlie; (4) Annie; (5) W. J.; (6) Vernon.

(*g*) Sallie, a twin to Willie (b. November 22d, 1869), married William McGaughey; issue: (1) Granville; (2) William; (3) Charlie; (4) Troy; (5) Vernella.

(*h*) James Elliott (b. October 22d, 1857), married Margaret Welch; issue, Mary Ethel.

(h) Helen (d. 1893), married Lazenby (d.) of Mississippi; issue:

(*a*) William, married ——; issue, eleven children.

(*b*) George, married ——; issue seven children.

(*c*) Mattie, married Davis Barron of Stein's Creek, Miss., and has five children.

(*d*) Edward, died 1890.

(*e*) Fannie, died s. p.

(*f*) Alice, died s. p.

(*g*) Ella (d. 1897), married John F. Chappell; issue, John, b. 1895.

(7) Sarah, daughter of Frank and —— (Booth) Stubbs, married John F. Mitchell of Putnam county, Georgia.

(8) Elizabeth, married Richmond Gore of Putnam county, Ga. A son of this union lived in Chicago and litigated the estate of Frank Stubbs in Utica, Miss.

(9) Nancy, married Isham Kendrick, and both died in Smith county, Texas.

(10) Catherine, married D. G. Rutledge of Harris county, Ga.

(11) Maria, married Willis Childs, and died in Butler county, Ala.

(12) Mary Stubbs, died an old maid in Macon county, Ala.

III. MILDRED SCOTT, born September 28th, 1775, died July 23d, 1825, as per tombstone, which reads:

> Mildred Scott Stubbs,
> Relict of Major Edward White,
> Born September 28th, 1775;
> Died July 23d, 1825.

Married Major Edward White, born at Brookline, Mass., 1758, died Jan. 9th, 1812; buried in cemetery at Savannah. He was in Revolutionary Army, and the following, taken from Heitman's Historical Register, gives his rank:

"Ensign Ninth Massachusetts, 1st July, 1777; Second Lieutenant, 6th March, 1778; transferred to Eighth Massachusetts 1st January, 1781; transferred to Third Massachusetts 12th June, 1783, and served to November 3d, 1783. Died 9th January, 1812."

Colonel (afterwards Brigadier General) Michael Jackson commanded the Eighth Massachusetts Regiment, and Capt. Burnham was his captain, and it is said that General Washington complimented this regiment on being the best disciplined one in the army (1778). Major White was present at the surrender of Burgoyne, 1777. After 1785 he went to Savannah Ga.; was ordinary of Chatham county and Collector of Port of Savannah (appointed by President Madison) until his death, in 1812. Issue of Mildred Scott Stubbs and Major Edward White:

(1) Dr. Benjamin A., of Milledgeville, Ga., "a man of high character and of great distinction in his profession;" married ——, and had:
    (a) Thomas, married Henrietta Kenan, daughter of A. H. Kenan of Milledgeville.

(2) Thomas, first of Cahaba, Ala., afterwards of Mobile. "A man of promise, but took to drink and died early."

(3) Maria Susan (d. December 22d, 1854), married, in Milledgeville, November 1st, 1825, Francis Vincent Deloney (died April 14th at the old Stubbs place near Milledgeville, Ga.). Issue:
    (a) James Edward, born August 22d, 1826, died young.
    (b) Francis Le Bourdais (b. March 11th, 1828, d. 1862), married, 1856, Anne Gachet; no issue.
    (c) Emily Mildred (b. April 24th, 1830), married James Hersey Nesbitt, and had issue.

(d) Pauline Virginia (b. November 8th, 1831), married LaFayette Carrington, and has a son a Colonel, another Captain of Marines and a third Surgeon in the United States Army.

(e) Jane Eleanor White, b. January 5th, 1834.

(f) Maria Susan, b. April 24th, 1837.

(g) George Gilmer, b. July 9th, 1839.

(h) Edward White, b. December 23d, 1841.

(i) Cephalia, b. April 6th, 1844.

IV. WILLIAM (b. 1777), married ——, and moved to Jones county, Ga., and had issue:

(1) James, married Angelina Bivens.

(2) Austin, married Miss Griswold, and had:

(a) James W., of Marrs Postoffice, Lowndes county, Ga.; married, and has Charles, of Macon, Ga., and perhaps others.

It is to be regretted that no further information could be obtained of William's descendants.

V. ELIZABETH (b. 1781), married Richard Ellis; issue:

(1) John, died s. p.

(2) Monroe, died s. p.

(3) Madison, died s. p.

(a) Sarah Lou, married Thos. P. Stubbs (see page 70).

VI. SARAH (b. 1783), married Lindsay Coleman; issue:

(1) Frances, married — Marshall, and lived near Augusta, Ga.

(2) Clara, married Robert D. Ware, and lived Augusta Ga.

(3) Lindsay, married Lizzie Winter, and lived near Augusta, Ga.

VII. LUCINDA (b. 1785), married Thomas Stubbs (b. 1783), son of Peter and Mary Baradall (Palmer) Stubbs. (See Thomas Stubbs, p. 66.)

VIII. JAMES EDWARD (b. 1787, d. 1824), married Martha Corley, and moved to Montgomery, Ala., in 1818. Issue:

(1) James Edward (b. 1814), married a Spanish lady, and died in Punta Rosa, Fla., leaving one daughter.

(2) Mary Ann (b. 1816, d. 1868), married Charles Black of Galveston, Texas; issue:

(a) William, died s. p.

(b) Charlotte, died s. p.

(c) Ellen, married Thomas Grout of Newport, Vt., and has two children, Charles and Addie Lou.

(3) Isham Baytop (b. March 6th, 1818, d. February 17th, 1901), of Montgomery, Ala.; married, January 7th, 1841, Mary Ann Conolly Saunders of Virginia (d. 1898); issue:
(a) James Edward (b. November 5th, 1841), unmarried.
(b) Thomas Baytop (b. October 12th, 1843), married, November 10th, 1870, Harriet A. Patillo; issue:
(a) Mary Oslin (b. 1871), married Mericott Warren Walker of Selma, Ala., and has Mericott W., b. 1890, and Erin, b. 1895.
(b) Ella Bertha (b. 1874), married, 1896, Ed. M. Johnson of Montgomery; no issue.
(c) Hattie Patillo (b. 1877), married, 1901, Walter Marion Ross, son of Wiley C. and Mary (Thomas) Ross of Lee county, Ala.
(c) Charles Henry, b. 1844, d. 1848.
(d) Mary Virginia, b. 1848, d. 1850.
(e) Robert Courtenay (b. 1851, d. 1898), married Emma Simpson (d. 1897) of Madison county, Ala.; no issue.
(f) Bertha Hansford (b. 1854), married, 1880, Edwin F. Jones, a prominent lawyer of Montgomery; issue:
(a) Samuel Baytop, b. 1884.
(b) Mary Virginia, b. 1888.
(g) George Marion, b. 1856, d. 1885, s. p.
(h) William Saunders, b. 1860, unmarried.
(i) Ada Elinor, b. 1867, d. 1868.
(4) Theodore Barancas, of Galveston, Texas (b. 1823, d. 1896), Colonel in C. S. A., a man of wealth and importance; married twice; first, Ellen Kirkpatrick of Montgomery, Ala.; had issue:
(a) James Baytop, graduate Washington and Lee University; city attorney of Galveston; b. 1850; married, 1876, R. Janie Allen; issue, three children: (a) Janie Allen, b. 1877; (b) James Baytop, b. 1878; (c) Lillian, b. 1882, d. 1883.
Second, married Kate Kaufman of Galveston, Texas; issue:
(b) John Andrew (b. 1856), married, 1889, Jennie McDonald; issue: (a) Frank Spencer, b. 1893; (b) Flora Arden, b. 1895.
(c) Theodore Bonaparte (b. 1857), married, 1885, Catherine Delehanty; issue: (a) Alice, b. 1886; (b) Lettie, b. 1887; (c) Theodore B., b. 1888; (d) Kate, b. 1889; (e) Cora, b. 1892; (f) Sidney, b. 1897; (g) William, b. 1900.

(d) Lillie, b. 1860, d. 1880.
(e) William J., b. 1862, d. 1866.
(f) Peter P., b. 1865, d. 1866.
(g) Charles J. b. 1867, lawyer and partner of brother James.
(h) Kate (b. 1870), married, 1892, Alfred Henry Dunkerly, cashier Ennis National Bank, Ennis, Texas; issue:
  (a) Marie Adele, b. 1895; (b) Kathryn Teresa, b. 1897.
(i) Adele Lubbock (b. 1872), married, 1898, Robert Lee McMahon; no issue.
(j) Henrietta, b. 1877.

IX. THOMAS BAYTOP (b. 1789, d. 1863), moved from Wilkes county, Ga., to Milledgeville, Ga., in 1805, and there amassed a fortune, and in 1845 moved to Tippah county, Miss., where he died. He married, 1810, Kate Palmer Stubbs, daughter of Peter and Mary Baradall (Palmer) Stubbs; issue:
(1) Mary Ann, born 1813, died, 1898, in Montgomery, Ala.; married Elliott C. Hannon; issue:
(a) Thomas Baytop, b. 1836, d. 1843.
(b) Elliott C., b. 1838, d. 1843.
(c) James Henry, b. 1840, d. 1842.
(d) Thomas Elliott (b. 1843, d. 1891), C .S. A., married Sallie Gilmer; issue:
  (a) George Gilmer, b. 1867.
  (b) Elliott C. (b. 1870), married Maria Founce; issue, Margaret.
  (c) Mary, b. 1874.
  (d) Caroline, b. 1876.
  (e) Louisa, b. 1880.
  (f) Joan, b. 1882.
(e) Rev. John Hannon, of San Francisco, Cal., a distinguished minister in M. E. Church, South (b. 1845), married Lucy Hall; issue:
  (a) Helen, b. 1894.
  (b) Elliott C., b. 1896.
(f) Charles Francis (b. 1848), married Mattie Gilmer; issue:
  (a) Pauline W., b. 1878.
  (b) Francis M., b. 1883.
  (c) Mattie Gilmer, b. 1887.
(g) William W., b. 1850, d. 1871 s. p.
(h) Benjamin W., b. 1817.
(2) Sarah Mildred, b. 1817, married Rev. Richard Mosley of North Mississippi; issue:

(a) Kate, married Dr. S. A. Walker of Baldwyn, Miss., and has issue.

(b) Sarah, married Dr. Banks.

(c) Dorothy.

(3) Thomas Baytop, born 1820, died 1897, in Henderson Tenn.; married Virginia Lenora Marks (d. 1896); issue:

(a) Thomas Francis, secretary Morgan Hardy Grain Co., Union City, Tenn.

(b) Sallie.

(c) Edward B. (b. 1867), married, 1897, Kate Townsend of Birmingham, Ala. He is agent K. C., M. & B. R. R. at Bessemer, Ala.

(d) Mary, married Robert E. McKinney, cashier Farmers and Merchants Bank of Henderson, Tenn.

(4) Charles Andrew (b. 1822), married Bettie Emory and has a son (and perhaps others), Thomas, of Ripley, Miss.

(5) Francis H. (b. 1825), married Nancy C. Kelley; issue:

(a) James T. (b. 1869), of Dallas, Texas; married ——.

(b) Henry, died young.

(c) William Francis (b. 1873), of Mascautah, Ill.; married ——, and has a daughter, Catherine.

(d) Richard Baytop, of Grand Prairie, Texas, married ——, and has Francis Mumford.

(e) John L., of Grand Prairie, Texas, insurance agent.

(f) George P., of Cuero, Texas.

(g) Elizabeth C., of Henderson, Tenn.

(h) Jennie S., of Grand Prairie, Texas.

(6) Henry Augustus (b. 1827), married Sarah Emory, and has a son (and perhaps others), Henry, of Ripley, Tenn.

(7) Rev. Benjamin White (b. 1832), M. E. Church, South; killed by a falling tree. Married Anna Barber; issue:

(a) Thomas Baytop, married ——.

(b) Edward, married – —.

(c) Benjamin, married ——.

There is a John Stubbs of Grand Prairie, Texas, a son of one of the above.

X. CAROLINE MATILDA (b. 1791), married Benjamin Gachet, son of Dr. Charles Gachet by first wife (Miss Scott); issue:

(1) Charles Benjamin, married Mary Morton.

(2) Louisa, married — Herston.

(3) Eliza, married A. B. Shehee.

(4) Mary, married — Milner.

# DESCENDANTS OF PETER AND MARY BARADELL (PALMER) STUBBS.

PETER, born June 1st, 1744, in Virginia, died 1821 in Putnam county, Ga.; married, 1776, widow of Louis Tyler, *nee* Mary Baradall Palmer (d. 1804). The following has been furnished by Hon. Lyon G. Tyler, President of William and Mary College, and son of John Tyler, President of the United States:

(1) John Tyler (d. 1773), married Anne Contesse, daughter of Dr. Louis Contesse, and had:

    (a) John (Governor of Virginia), who was father of President Tyler.

    (b) Lewis (d. 1775), married Mary Baradall Palmer.

(2) Mary (d. 1789), married, 1745, Rev. William Preston (b. 1719, d. 1778).

(3) Edith, married Rev. Thomas Robinson.

(4) Joanna, married Dr. Kenneth McKenzie.

(5) Elizabeth Lowe, married, first, Bowcock (d. 1746); married, second (1753), John Palmer (d. 1760), a lawyer and bursar of William and Mary College, Virginia.

In 1775 Governor John Tyler advertised sale of brick house, near Capitol, belonging to daughters of late John Palmer. Lewis Tyler was a lawyer and lived in Charlotte county at "Red Hill," afterwards the home of Patrick Henry. From above it appears that Lewis Tyler married his cousin, Mary Baradall Palmer, daughter of his Aunt Elizabeth Lowe Tyler. It is probable that the mother of John Palmer was a Baradall.

The following is taken from the Charlotte county (Va.) records:

*Will of Lewis Tyler.*—I, Lewis Tyler, of Charlotte county, very low and weak though in perfect senses, do make my last will and testament. Item: My will and desire is that the land I purchased upon Turnip Creek to be sold to relieve my securities of the said land, which land was purchased of John Rogers and Robert Caldwell, which was the property of Robert Daugherty. The residue of my estate, after my debts are paid, I give and bequeath unto my wife, Mary Baradall Tyler. I leave my brother John Tyler, Richard M. Booker and Peter Stubbs executors.

June 30th, 1775.

his<br>LEWIS  +  TYLER.<br>mark

Witnesses: Peter Stubbs, Richard Booker, Joanna Tyler.

At a Court held for Charlotte county 1st day of September, 1777, the above written last will and testament of Lewis Tyler, deceased, was exhibited in Court by Peter Stubbs, one of his executors therein named, and the same was proved by oath of Joanna Bouldin, one of the witnesses thereto subscribed, and ordered to be certified, and the said Peter Stubbs renouncing in open Court the execution of said will and it appearing that Richard Marot Booker renounces the execution of said will, as also John Tyler, the other executor, as by his letter this day read in Court; therefore on the motion of George Caldwell, with the assent of Peter Stubbs and Mary, his wife, administration with the will annexed of the estate of said Louis Tyler, deceased, is granted him, he making oath according to law and giving security, whereupon he, together with Robert Caldwell, his security, entered into and acknowledged their bond for this purpose. Test: THOS. READ, Clerk.

At a Court for Charlotte county the 6th day of October, 1777, the above written last will and testament of Lewis Tyler, deceased. was further proved by the oath of Richard Marricott Booker, one of the witnesses hereto subscribed, and ordered to be recorded. Test., Tho. Read, C.

Fully recorded          THO. REED, C. C.
Copy Teste, J. C. Carrington, C.

Peter, after marrying the Widow Tyler, moved from Virginia to Wilkes county, Georgia, probably about 1783. Smith in his "History of Georgia" says he came 1787 to 1793, along with John, Sylvester and Abner Hammond. He moved from Elbert (taken from Wilkes) to Putnam, where he died in 1821. Of Mrs. Stubbs it is said, "She suffered during the Revolution with smallpox, from the effects of which she went blind. It is said that she never saw but one (John, the eldest) of her children. She was very diminutive and wore No. 13 shoes." Letter from Miss Kate Palmer Stubbs.)

The children of Peter and Mary Baradall (Palmer) Stubbs were:

I. JOHN, born April 12, 1777, in Virginia, died in Franklin county, Ga., and is buried four miles east of Carnesville, Ga.; married, in 1807, Ann Upshur of Elbert county; issue, seven children. (see forward page.)

II. THOMAS, born August 18th, 1783, died in Bibb county, Ga.; married, 1809, Lucinda, daughter of James and Mary

Eliza (Scott) Stubbs; issue, six children. (See forward page.)

III. JAMES, born January 18th, 1785. He must have died young, as no knowledge of him can be found beyond the record of his birth in the family Bible.

IV. CATHERINE PALMER, born March 19th, 1788; married, 1810, Thomas Baytop Stubbs, son of James and Mary Eliza (Scott) Stubbs of Elbert county, Ga. He had moved to Milledgeville in 1805, and after acquiring wealth moved to Tippah county, Miss., in 1845, where they died. (See issue under Thomas Baytop Stubbs, see page 55.)

V. FRANCIS, born November 7th, 1791, of Putnam county, Ga. Moved to Bibb county, where he died March 3, 1858. Married, 1813, Martha Moody (b. 1793, d. 1872); issue, nine children. (See forward page.)

VI. MILDRED SCOTT, born January 18th, 1793; married, first (1812), James Fleming, and went to Mississippi in 1845; issue:
(1) Thomas, who married a widow and left no issue.
(2) Antonette, married a Lane and had a son who was Presbyterian minister in North Mississippi, and he had Edward and other children.
Mildred Scott married, second, Emnior Bayles, and had no issue.

VII. PETER, JR., born May 8th, 1796; married, 1820, Ann Hammond, and lived and died in Bibb county, Ga.; issue, thirteen children. (See forward page.)

VIII. BARADALL PALMER, born February 3d, 1799, in Elbert county, Ga.; married, January 30th, 1823, in Milledgeville, Ga., Eliza Hammond (b. October 20th, 1805, in Louisville, Ga.). He died in Macon, Ga., October 17th, 1873. Issue, eleven children. (See forward page.)

## DESCENDANTS OF JOHN AND ANN (UPSHUR) STUBBS.

I. MARY PALMER, born December 12th, 1808, died April 4th, 1859; married, October 9th, 1828, John F. Wilson (b. 1808, d. 1858) of Campbell county, Ga.; issue:

(1) Mary Ann (b. September 12th, 1829, d.), married Frank Pitts; issue: (a) Ella; (b) Augustus; (c) Mildred; all living in Texas.

(2) John Stubbs (b. February 14th, 1831, d.), married Amantha Gilbert; issue: (a) Mollie; (b) John; (c) William; (d) Walter; (e) Hattie; (f) Mattie.

(3) Sarah Mildred (b. April 13th, 1833, d.), married John F. Maclaren; issue (a) Eddie; (b) John, d.

(4) Mahulda C. (b. March 23d, 1835, d), married Dr. J. T. Davenport; issue: (a) Thomas, d.; (b) Charles.

(5) William Leak (b. January 30th, 1840), married Kate E. Hornsby, daughter of Dr. J. Hornsby (P. O., Maude, Ga.); issue: (a) Lola, married R. J. Maclean, issue Lola Wilson; (b) Olive, married R. J. MacDougall, issue Donald and Robert Leake; (c) Claude; (d) Frank; (e) Kate; (f) Nellie May; (g) Miller.

(6) Henrietta E. (b. April 18th, 1842), married, first, Dr. William Williams and, second, Looney Redwine. Issue by first husband: (a) John Thomas. By second husband: (b) William; (c) Hill; (d) Charles.

(7) James M. (b. May 18th, 1844, d.), married Adeline Longino, daughter of Tom Longino; issue: (a) Minnie; (b) Richard, d.; (c) Fanny Lowe, d.; (d) James M.; (e) Dorsey.

(8) Frances E. (b. March 23d, 1846), married George F. Longino; issue: (a) Cecil; (b) John; (c) Earnest; (d) Lovick; (e) Bessie; (f) Fannie.

(9) Alexander H. (b. July 3d, 1848), married Carrie Hornsby (d.); issue: (a) Forest; (b) Inez; (c) Leake; (d) Alexander; (e) Penn; (f) Jewel; (g) Lowe; (h) Carl; (i) De Witt.

(10) Samuel A. (b. October 23d, 1850), married Victoria Hornsby; issue: (a) Estelle, d.; (b) Herbert; (c) Edwin; Chandler, d.
(d) Maude; (e) Fay; (f) Effie; (g) Willard; (h)

II. SARAH THOMAS, born August 7th, 1813, in Franklin county, Ga., died August 4th, 1836; married, October 6th, 1831, James H. Wilson (b. 1810); issue:

(1) Nancy Leake, born October 21st, 1832, died in Campbell county, Ga., July 21st, 1869; married, February 19th, 1861, William H. Ferguson; issue:

(a) Mattie T: (b. November 18th, 1861), of Atalnta, Ga.

(b) Wm. H., of Atlanta, Ga. (b. September 23d, 1862); married Ruth Pierce, granddaughter of Bishop George Pierce; issue: (*a*) Leslie; (*b*) Mary; (*c*) William.

(c) Sarah F., b. July 21st, 1863.

(2) Martha Caroline (b. October 25th, 1834), married (second wife), January 13th, 1875, Stephen Collins of Macon, Ga.; no issue. There were eight children by first wife.

(3) Sarah Francis, b. November 18th, 1835, d. July 29th, 1857.

III. JOHN UPSHUR (d. 1849), married Martha P. Wilson; issue:

(1) Capt. John Smith (42d Georgia Regiment, C. S. A.), of Cedarton, Polk county, Ga.; for sketch of service and life see Confederate Military History, pages 988-990; married, September 15th, 1867, Madge A. Simmons of Cave Springs, Ga.; issue:

(a) Eula L., b. July 4th, 1868.

(b) John V., of Dalton, Ga., b. April 8th, 1872.

(c) Marie M., b. May 22d, 1874.

(d) William H., b. February 24th, 1876; Secretary and Treasurer of Atlantic and Gulf Manufacturing Company, Quitman, Ga.

(e) Albert W., of Cedarton, b. November 26th, 1880.

(f and g) Mattie F. and Madge S. (twins), b. October 26th, 1882.

(h) Edgar A., b. March 23d, 1884.

(2) Thomas Baradall, of Bird's Station, Ala. (b. August 23d, 1843), married, December, 1863, Laura Hughes; issue: (a) John W.; (b) Lee W.; (c) Dora.

IV. CATHERINE PALMER (d. 1845), married, 1840, John Adderhold of Franklin county, Ga.; issue:

(1) Mary.

(2) Sarah.

V. JAMES FRANKLIN, b. September 30th, 1811, d. August 2d, 1871, in De Kalb county, Ga.; married three times; first (1836), Nancy Adams; issue, three children:

(1) Ann (b. December 5th, 1837), married, 1855, Benjamin F. Morris and moved to Purley, Texas, where they now live; issue:

  (a) John Franklin (b. October 26th, 1856), married, January 13th, 1880, Rebecca Thompson; issue, eight children.

  (b) Watt (b. December 11th, 1858, d. 1895), married, 1880, Emma Birdsong; issue, six children.

  (c) Lula (b. February 23d, 1861), married, 1880, W. B. Denny (d. 1887), no issue; married, second (1882), L. Hedrick; issue, six children.

  (d) James Benjamin (b. February 12th, 1866), married, 1894, Vina Smith; issue, three children.

  (e) Georgia (b. December 7th, 1867), married, 1894, Westbrook.

  (f) Garrett A. (b. July 19th, 1870), unmarried.

  (g) Dolly (b. March 9th, 1872), married, 1901), Mr. Butler; issue, one child.

  (h) Elijah (b. August 1st, 1874), married, 1896, Laura Williamson; issue, two children.

  (i) Pinkie (b. March 30th, 1876), married, 1898, Mr. Perryman; issue, three children.

  (j) Earnest Stubbs, b. Nov. 12th, 1878.

(2) James Arnold, of Fairburn, Ga., b. April 25th, 1838 (C. S. A.); married, December 12th, 1868, Sallie Varner Spear; issue:

  (a) Dr. George Hamilton, of Birmingham, Ala., married, April 12th, 1899, Mary Adele Rucker, daughter of Gen. E. W. Rucker, a distinguished Confederate soldier.

  (b) Arnold Whitfield, of Virginia, a traveling salesman.

  (c) Elizabeth.

  (d) Jemmy Lowe.

  (e) Nancy Adams.

  (f) Willie.

(3) George, b. January, 2d, 1840, Lieutenant C. S. A., and killed at Winchester, Va., June 28th, 1864.

JAMES FRANKLIN married, second, Ladoska Calloway (d. 1860) of Henry county, Ga.; issue:

  (4) Sallie, married A. S. Poole of Atlanta, Ga.; issue: (a) Lola; (b) Thomas; (c) Jennie, died young; (d) Leake, died young; (e) Lamar; (f) William; (g) Earnest.

  (5) Nancy, married Dr. Samuel Wilson of Fulton county, and died s. p.

  (6) John Franklin, of East Atlanta (b. 1848), married Mat-

tie Morris of De Kalb county, Ga.; issue, ten children, viz.: (a) James; (b) Pearl; (c) Calloway; (d) Gustavus; (e) Nannie Lou; (f) Mattie Bell; (g) Charles; (h) Ruth; and two others.

(7) William Donald (b. 1852, d. November, 1894), married Emma Cobb; issue: (a) Edna; (b) Ruby; (c) Annie; (d) Frank.

(8) Laura, married John Poole, and lives in South Atlanta; issue: (a) May; (b) Gertrude; (c) Crandall; (d) Janie; (e) Nettie; (f) Sallie; (g) John; (h) Annie; (i) Thomas.

JAMES FRANKLIN STUBBS, married, third, March 3d, 1863, Martha Corley of Monroe county, Ga.; issue:

(9) Fannie V., married Marcus Brown of Bremen, Ga.; issue: (a) Florence, b. September 7th, 1888; (b) Ruth Early, b. March 2d, 1890; (c) Marcus L., b. February 18th, 1892; (d) James Stubbs, b. September 30th, 1894; (e) Robert Toombs, b. December 27th, 1896; (f) George Scott, b. November 8th, 1899.

(10) Charles O. (b. September 5th, 1867), married, July 8th, 1888, Annie Colquitt Mitchell of Carroll county, Ga., and lives at Westminster, Texas, where he is President of Westminster College. He graduated at Bowdon College June, '87; Professor of Mathematics in Thomasville, Ga., '87-'90, Professor of Mathematics in Bowdon College '91-'92, and President of Bowdon College, '94-96. Issue:
(a) Harry D., b. August 17th, 1889;
(b) Mattie Beryl, b. October 13th, 1891, d. July 10th, 1898;
(c) Annie Belle, b. May 20th, 1901.

(11) Mattie Leake, died s. p.

VI. GEORGE W. (b. May 19th, 1815, d. October 19th, 1863), married, August 20th, 1840, Sarah A. McMullen (d. February 4th, 1866) of Bartow county, Georgia.; issue:

(1) John W., of Pine Log, Ga. (b. February 8th, 1844, married, December 17th, 1874, Savannah E. Stanford; issue, Dora Alberta, b. October 13th, 1875.

(2) Katherine A., b. April 1st, 1846, d. November 7th, 1846.

(3) Frances H. (b. October 2d, 1847), married J. T. Spearman of Chattanooga, Tenn. Residence, 301 Montgomery avenue.

(4) James S. (b. January 7th, 1850), of Comanche, Texas.

(5) Elizabeth T. (b. February 2d, 1852), of Pine Log, Ga.

(6) Sophie J., b. April 15th, 1854, d. July 28th, 1868.

(7) George L. (b. June 26th, 1856), of Chattanooga, Tenn.
(8) William Baradall (b. November 7th, 1859), of Tulip, Ga.

N. B.—It is to be regretted that no fuller information can be given of the above, but repeated letters evoked no responses, and hence the above information, obtained from Mr. John W. Stubbs of Pine Log, Ga., is all that can be given.—W. C. S.

VII. MATILDA CAROLINE (b. May 14th, 1825, d. August 20th, 1886), married, August 15th, 1843, Jacob Weems (b. 1813, d. 1894). Both died in Chambers county, Ala, and left issue:
    (1) Sarah A. E. (b. June 28th, 1844), married, November 17th, 1867, F. M. Norton (d. 1873).
    (2) James A. Weems (b. October 22d, 1846), married, December 7th, 1871, Malinda Bell.
    (3) Martha C. b. November 19th, 1849, d. July 31st, 1887, in Cherokee county, Ala.; married, August 27th, 1870, R. T. Sharp (d. 1898).
    (4) William R., b. March 30th, 1854, d. July 2d, 1870.
    (5) Thomas E. Mc D. (b. May 1st, 1856), married, September 7th, 1879, Frances Baxter.
    (6) Mary J. E. (b. October 29th, 1858), married, December 27th, 1882, R. A. Ritch.
    (7) Carrie F. (b. July 25th, 1860), married ——.
    (8) Lodosky H. (b. July 25th, 1862, d. August 7th, 1885), married, December 27th, 1882, A. L. Ritch.

## DESCENDANTS OF THOMAS AND LUCINDA
## (STUBBS) STUBBS.

I. THOMAS PETER (d. August 4th, 1859), a distinguished lawyer in Macon, Ga.; married Rebecca Lundy; issue:
> (1) Eliza, died s. p.; (2) Robert W., died s. p.; (3) Walter,
> died s. p.; (4) Clarence, died s. p.

II. CATHERINE PALMER (d. May 5th, 1850), married Washington Saunders. Issue:
> (1) Lucinda, married Barfield; issue, three children.
> (2) Emma, married Barfield, issue, four children.
> (3) Rebecca Eliza (b. March 4th, 1850), married, 1875,
> William Robinson; issue, eight children.

III. CAROLINE SARAH MATILDA (b. 1819, d. 1885), married,
1834, Jesse Joly Kennedy (d. 1855); issue:
> (1) James Benjamin (b. 1849), of Lowe, Macon county,
> Ga.; married, November 19th, 1874, Elizabeth Agee;
> issue: (a) Jesse M., b. January 4th, 1876; (b) Mary, b.
> 1880; (c) Annie, b. August 8th, 1881; (d) Benjamin, b.
> October 22d, 1885; (e) Edward Stubbs, b. March 10th,
> 1887; (f) Sarah Mildred, b. January 4th, 1890.

IV. JAMES A., b. February 28th, 1815, in Jones county, Ga.. d.
April 17th, 1889; married, first (October 14th, 1846), Mary
Julia Bentz; second (December 18th, 1855), Caroline Elizabeth
Bentz, daughters of George Bentz of Houston county, Georgia.
Issue by first wife (none by second):
> (1) George Peter, Mercht, of Cochran, Ga. (b September
> 20th, 1847, d. March 21st, 1895), married, April 8th, 1883,
> Ada Brown of Cochran, Pulaski county, Ga.; issue: (a)
> Julia, b. May 18th, 1884; (b) Frank, b. March 16th, 1886;
> (c) Lucy, b. December 27th, 1889; (d) James, b. August
> 10th, 1891.
> (2) Eliza Louise (b. November 19th, 1849), married, in
> Sumter county, Ga., November 14th, 1878, W. W. Linch
> of Linchburg, Putnam county, Ga., a farmer and mer-
> chant; issue: (a) Julia May, b. May 21st, 1880; (b)
> James Wilkin, b. October 4th, 1882; (c) William Stubbs,
> b. April 25th, 1885; (d) Emma Ethel, b. January 20th,
> 1888; (e) John Carl, b. September 2d, 1890.
> (3) Margaret Caroline (b. June 8th, 1853), married, in
> Jacksonville, Fla., February, 1889, Hiram T. Mann of Wil-
> liston, Fla., a farmer.

V. EDWARD WHITE (d. October 31st, 1884), married Mary
Bronson of Macon, Ga.; issue:

(1) James Horace of Huntington, Ga. (b. January 22d, 1848), married, December 8th, 1868, Annie E. Finch (b. November 27th, 1849; issue:

(a) Lucy Ann (b. September 21st, 1869), married, January 8th, 1888, William J. Cordell; issue: (*a*) Walter Roy, b. November 9th, 1888; (*b*) Berdit Carl, b. December 22d, 1889; (*c*) William Cecil, b. December 27th, 1895.

(b) Oscar Palmer (b. June 22d, 1871), married, December 23d, 1896, Annie L. Folds; issue, Willa Lee, b. February 16th, 1898.

(c) Albert Clifton (b. August 16th, 1873), married, February 16th, 1897, Mattie Love Morgan (d. February 15th, 1898) ; issue, Mattie Eunice, b. February 1st, 1898.

(d) Ella Alberta, b. May 11th, 1875.

(e) Charles White, (b. February 2d, 1877, d. August 25th, 1878).

(f) Berdit Finch, b. January 19th, 1879.

(g) Mabel Finch, b. February 11th, 1882.

(h) Sarah Finch, b. March 23d, 1885.

(i) John Thornton, b. March 28th, 1887.

(j) Julia Inez, b. August 10th, 1890, d. July 31st, 1891.

(2) Baradall (b. 1849), married Sophronia Duncan of Taylor county, Ga.; issue: (a) Mary Lee; (b) Edward.

(3) Margaret Caroline (d. 1898), married Noah Taylor of Macon county, Ga.; issue, eight children.

(4) Julia Irene (d. 1899), married Thomas De Vene; issue, three children.

(5) Samuel (d. 1897), married Emma Robinson of Macon county, Ga.; issue, a daughter, Jewel.

VI. ANN ELIZA (d. January 17th, 1848), married (first wife) Wilson C. Hardy; issue, Lucy, married James Cowart of Macon, Ga. Mr. Hardy married, second, Martha Ann Stubbs, daughter of Frank and Martha (Moody) Stubbs. (For issue see page 73.)

## DESCENDANTS OF FRANCIS AND MARTHA (MOODY) STUBBS.

I. JAMES JOHN, born February 18th, 1814, killed by a slave 1856; married, August 21st, 1834, Elizabeth J. Davis (d. 1871) of Lee county, Ga.; issue:

(1) James Francis, b. December 1st, 1836, unmarried.

(2) Henry Augustus, b. January 28th, 1838, d. s. p.

(3) Thomas Jefferson, b. December 1st, 1840, d. June 8th, 1891, from wound received in C. S. A.; married, November 22d, 1862, Mary E. Griggs; issue:

(a) Susan Rebecca (b. November 29th, 1865), married, November 30th, 1887, Franklin S. Pierce; issue: (*a*) Mary Thomas, b. Sept. 2d, 1888; (*b*) John Edward, b. August 22d, 1890; (*c*) William Franklin, b. October 8th, 1891; (*d*) Augustus, b. January 17th, 1894; (*e*) Chester Waldron, b. September 11th 1895.

(b) Edward Francis, of Bonaire, Ga. (b. November 29th, 1863), married, September 2d, 1890, Mary Ammons; issue: (*a*) James Wesley, b. July 27th, 1891; (*b*) Millard Francis, b. January 26th, 1893, died young; (*c*) Joseph Franklin, b. July 16th, 1894; (*d*) Edward May, b. February 14th, 1898; (*e*) Ethel Burruss, b. May 15th, 1900.

(c) Elizabeth E. (b. June 15th, 1874), married, September 10th, 1893, John R. Ammons of Welston, Houston county, Ga.; issue: Susie Claire, b. July 12th, 1897, and William Frank and Beaumont Earl, both dying young.

(4) Susan Eugene (b. January 8th, 1843) (d.), married Thomas Pearson (d.); no issue.

(5) Olive Gabriella (b. July 29th, 1846), married Avery Buckner of Eatonton, Ga.; issue: (a) Gussie, (b) Elizabeth, (c) Susie, (d) Louise, (e) John, (f) Edward.

(6) Charles Hambleton (b. Oct. 1st, 1848), of Note, Ga.; married Phosie Maddox; issue: (a) Ernest, (b) Mabel.

(7) Alonza (b. Aug. 29th, 1857), died in Texas, s. p.

(8) Robt. Davis Stubbs (b. April 9th, 1854), married at Eatonton, Ga., Maude Middleton; issue:

(a) Roy Davis, graduate University of Georgia and now special agent U. S. Dept. of Agriculture, in charge of Experiment Station at Cairo, Ga.

(b) Ethel (d.)

II. ELIZABETH ANN (b. Jan. 18th, 1816, d. 1817).

III. WM. BARADALL (b. Feb. 5th, 1818, d. July 20th, 1865), married, Feb. 1st, 1840, Martha Jane Davis (b. 1827, d. 1897), of Putnam county, Georgia. They moved to Abbeville, Wilcox county, Georgia, in 1861; issue:

(1) Mary Amanda (b. Oct. 8th, 1841), married, December, 1852, A. A. T. Reed of Virginia (d. 1900); issue:
  (a) Belle (b. Dec. 9th, 1865, d. Nov. 6th, 1892), married Jan. 5th, 1886, Dr. A. R. Royal; issue: (a) Rebecca born April 1st, 1887; (b) A. R., Jr., born Sept. 10th, 1890; (c) Edward H., born Oct. 30th, 1894.
  (b) Jessie, died young.
  (c) Laura (b. Jan. 7th, 1870), married Aug. 28th, 1892, E. H. Williams of North Carolina, now of Abbeville, Ga.; issue: (a) Belle Reid, born July 2d, 1893; (b) Laura, born June, 1895; (c) Edward, born Oct. 3, 1897; (d) Charles, born Oct. 18th, 1899; (e) Wm. L., born Oct. 19th, 1901.
  (d) Fannie (b. Dec. 2d, 1867), married July 5th, 1894, Geo. Parrott of Fitzgerald, Ga.; issue: (a) Blakeley, born March 23d, 1895; (b) George, born December, 1896.
  (e) Virginia (b. Dec. 1st, 1871), married July, 1894, her brother-in-law, Dr. A. R. Royal (d. 1899); issue: (a) Virginia, born Feb. 10th, 1896; (b) Eunice, born Sept. 9th, 1898.
  (f) Wm. (b. July 1st, 1874), unmarried.
  (g) John L. (b. Nov. 20th, 1876), unmarried.
(2) Martha Frances (b. Nov. 20th, 1842), married Aug. 21st, 1854, John Clack of Bibb county, Georgia (d. 1884); issue:
  (a) Wm. Benj. (b. Oct. 8th, 1870, d. July 20th, 1899, s. p.)
  (b) Della (b. Sept. 18th, 1875, d. Sept. 17th, 1897, s. p.)
  (c) Sarah Jane (b. Sept. 12th, 1872), married Dec. 24th, 1899, J. A. Hunt of Abbeville, Ga.; issue: Albion, born Oct. 31st, 1900.
  (d) John James (b. Jan. 25th, 1880), died young.
(3) Elizabeth Ellen (b. July 4th, 1854), married, 1868, John MacCartney (d. 1900) of Abbeville, Ga. (father from Ireland); issue: (a) Wm. Hugh (b. March 8th, 1875); (b) Annie (b. Dec. 21st, 1877); (c) Thomas (b. Feb. 18th, 1878); (d) Nettie (b. Jan. 22d, 1884); (e) Janie (b. Feb. 14th, 1887)
(4) Carrie Lou (b. Feb. 18th, 1860), married Feb. 18th,

1879, Benj. McAnally of Abbeville, Ga.; issue: (a) Edna (b. Sept. 1st, 1883); (b) Virginia (b. Feb. 22d, 1887); (c) James Arnold (b. July 21st, 1893); (d) John Stubbs (b. October, 1895); (e) Sarah Jane (b. May 21st, 1898); (f) Susie Bennie (b. Oct. 27th, 1900).
(5) Catherine Antoinette (b. Aug. 1st, 1850), unmarried.
(6) Wm. Alexander (b. Aug. 16th, 1846), unmarried.
(7) James Andrews (b. Sept. 12th, 1848), unmarried.
(8) Augustus Arnold (b. Jan. 31st, 1858), unmarried.

IV. CATHERINE ELIZABETH (b. Aug. 18th, 1820), married, first, in 1835, Mathew Farley, and second, W. J. Farley; no issue.

V. THOMAS P. (b. May 14th, 1822, d. 1864), married Oct. 25th, 1847, Sarah Washington. She lives now in north Georgia. Issue:
(1) Alpheus Beverly (b. July 12th, 1849).
(2) Robt. A. F. (b. Nov. 9th, 1852).
(3) Homer (b.——).

VI. GEORGE HENRY (b. July 1st, 1824, d. April 4th, 1896), married Sept. 2d, 1844, Susan Wesley Bowdoin (b. Feb. 2d, 1827, d. Aug. 28th, 1900), at Andersonville, Ga.; issue:
(1) Elizabeth Catherine (b. Oct. 30th, 1845), married, first, John Graham Dougherty (b. 1847, d. 1876), of Sumter county, Georgia; issue:
   (a) George Arthur (b. July 20th, 1870), married May 20th, 1896, Mildred Connie (b. 1877); issue: (*a*) Charles, born April 15th, 1897; (*b*) Ola A., born Jan. 13th, 1899.
   (b) Charles Virgie (b. Oct. 14th, 1871), married Oct. 12th, 1899, Alma DeLillian Dickerson (b. 1877); issue: Emma Mae, born July 28th, 1900.
   (c) Ola A. (b. 1874, d. 1875).
   (d) Jessie Michall (b. 1876, d. 1884).
She married, second, April 6th, 1882, P. B. Freeman of Macon, Ga., who was killed by a locomotive Oct. 27th, 1884; issue:
   (e) Roe (b. March 6th, 1883).
(2) Georgia Ann (b. May 31st, 1847, d. Sept. 17th, 1849).
(3) Daniel Hambleton (b. Jan. 7th, 1849), married December, 1894, Virginia Petersburg Brown (b. 1850). They reside near Americus, Ga. No issue.
(4) George Whitfield (b. Oct. 29th, 1850, d. July, 1900),

married March 15th, 1870, Maria L. Richards (b. 1852);
issue:
  (a) Annie Forest (b. Feb. 5th, 1871).
  (b) Lucy Elberta (b. Feb. 28th, 1873), died young.
  (c) Emmett Blue (b. Oct. 18th, 1874).
  (d) Mamie Lynn (b. June 18th, 1877).
  (e) Nellie Florence (b. March 22d, 1881), died young.
  (f) Homer Blanton (b. March 22d, 1883).
  (g) Samuel Hassam (b. June 25th, 1886).
  (h) Ruby Estelle (b. June 25th, 1890).
(5) Charles Franklin (b. May 3d, 1852, d. April 3d, 1868).
(6) Rev. Samuel Wesley, M. E. Church, South (b. Sept.
  12th, 1856, d. Jan. 4th, 1895), married Oct. 18th, 1883,
  Eugenia Capitola Dickey (b. 1859). She now lives at
  Cairo, Ga. Issue:
  (a) Myra Adele (b. March 16th, 1883), student at Wes-
      leyan Female College, Macon, Ga.
  (b) Lawrence Clements (b. Jan. 10th, 1886).
  (c) Susie Anna (b. April 20th, 1888).
  (d) Wm. Dickey (b. March 8th, 1893).
  (e) Samuel Eugenia (b. Aug. 27th, 1895).
(7) Mary Addie (b. March 4th, 1857), married Jan. 13th,
  1876, Thomas J. (Smith) Wicker of Macon, Ga. (b. 1848),
  a farmer and stockman near Americus, Ga; issue:
  (a) Mary Louisa (b. Dec. 10th, 1876), married March 3d,
      1901, Jas. Gordon Feagin (b. 1877).
  (b) William Francis (b. April 24th, 1878).
  (c) Alice Eula (b. Aug. 31st, 1880).
  (d) Geo. James (b. April 9th, 1883).
  (e) Chas. Horace (b. Oct. 30th, 1885, d. June 30th, 1887).
  (f) Annie May (b. Nov. 13th, 1888).
  (g) Laura Beulah (b. Dec. 8th, 1892).
  (h) Mattie Jewel (b. July 18th, 1898, d. Nov. 26th, 1901).
  (i) Arthur Grady (b. June, 1898).
  (j) Thomas Hamilton (b. Sept. 14th, 1900).
(8) Martha Francis (b. Feb. 16th, 1859), married April
  26th, 1888, to John F. Moreland, who resides on the old
  homestead of Geo. H. Stubbs, near Americus, Ga.; issue:
  (a) Nannie Sue (b. June 4th, 1889).
  (b) John Joseph (b. June 9th, 1890).
  (c) Carrie Eliza (b. Sept. 5th, 1891).
  (d) Mary Julia (b. Dec. 24th, 1892).
  (e) Robt. Hamilton (b. May 30th, 1894.)
  (f) Charles Wesley (b. Sept. 3d, 1895).
  (g) Martha Beulah (b. Dec. 31st, 1896).

(h) Willie Belle (b. Nov. 28th, 1899, d. Dec. 4th, 1899).

(9) Carrie Maria (b. Feb. 23d, 1861), married Feb. 3d, 1884, James Monroe (Smith) Wicker (b. 1860), of Oglethorpe, Ga.; issue:

(a) David (b. March 22nd, 1886).
(b) Samuel Wesley (b. May 11th, 1890).
(c) Carrie (b. June 10th, 1892).
(d) Watson (b. Nov. 30th, 1893).
(e) Jannie (b. Feb. 25th, 1896).
(f) Mary Dannie (b. Dec. 21st, 1898).

(10) Laura Belle (b. Jan. 6th, 1863), married Dec. 3d, 1886, Rev. Thos. W. Darley (b. 1858), of S. Ga. Conf. M. E. Church, South; issue:

(a) Thos. W. (b. Feb. 9th, 1897).
(b) Herbert S. (b. Dec. 29th, 1898).
(c) Susie Lamar (b. Aug. 29th, 1900).

He is now stationed at Quitman, Ga.

(11) Anna Beulah (b. Sept. 4th, 1864), married Nov. 19th, 1885, Fortune F. Farmer (b. 1858), of Blackarten, Devonshire, England, but now lives at Abbeville, Ga.; issue:

(a) Theodore William (b. Aug. 13th, 1889).
(b) Mattie Eugenia (b. Jan. 30th, 1891).
(c) Geo. Royal (b. June 27th, 1894).
(d) Howard LaNutt (b. April 15th, 1896).
(e) Ruth Antoinette (b. Aug. 31st, 1898).
(f) Chrystine (b. Dec. 25th, d. 1901).

(12) Julia Franklin (b. April 11th, 1866), married Sept. 10th, 1885, Jesse Lee Chambliss (b. 1865); issue:

(a) Annie Elizabeth (b. Nov. 20th, 1886).
(b) Jessie George (b. Jan. 30th, 1889).
(c) Wm. Lee (b. Jan. 31st, 1891).

Mr. Chambliss is in cotton commission business and a farmer of Americus, Ga.

(13) Robt. Henry (b. Dec. 29th, 1868), married Oct. 29th, 1896, Fannie C. Pennington (b. 1874); issue:

(a) Mary Alice (b. Aug. 28th, 1896).
(b) Robt. Samuel (b. Nov. 15th, 1898).
(c) Geo. Andrew (b. Nov. 25th, 1900).

He is a farmer near Andersonville. Ga.

VII. JOEL G. (b. May 14th, 1828, d. Jan. 1st, 1862), married May 16th, 1860, F. E. V. Tankersly; issue:

Joel Thomas (b. April 25th, 1861), married Mrs. Nettie (Cowart) Stubbs, widow of Thomas Stubbs, and had issue: Lela, Joel, and Albert.

VIII. MARY ANTONETTE (b. Sept. 2d, 1830, d. 1874), married, first wife, Nov. 17th, 1846, Thomas, son of Peter and Ann (Hammond) Stubbs (b. 1826, d. 1877) ; no issue. Thomas married, second, Nettie Cowart, and had issue: Thomas Peter (b. Dec. 25th, 1875), married Jan. 21st, 1900, Minnie Vinson (d. 1891). No issue.

After death of Thomas his widow married Joel Thomas Stubbs, as above.

IX. MARTHA ANN (b. March 14th, 1833), married, second wife, Jan. 21st, 1849, Wilson C. Hardy; issue:

(a) Frank Whitfield (b. Oct. 21st, 1849) Macon, Ga.; married Anna Ross.

(b) George.

(c) Mattie.

(d) Hattie.

(e) Seaborn Jones, and others.

## DESCENDANTS OF PETER AND ANN (HAMMOND) STUBBS.

I. PETER (b. Aug. 12th, 1821, d. 1822).

II. ABNER PALMER (b. Dec. 26th, 1822), married, 1845, Martha Ann Woodward; issue:
  (1) Lycurgus A. (b. 1847), a farmer in Bibb county, Georgia; married Susan Simmons; issue:
    (a) Wm. Abner, married Mollie Bacon; issue: (a) Frank, (b) Louisa.
    (b) Chas. T., married Susie Middlebrooks; issue: (a) Eugenia, (b) Bertha, (c) Kirkland.
    (c) Lulu, married L. E. Menshew; issue: (a) Russell, (b) an infant.
    (d) Joseph, married Nora Pierce; issue: one child.
    (e) Emma; (f) Katie; (g) Homer.
  (2) Peter Woodward (b. 1849), married, first, Mary Kemp (d. 1894), and lives at old homestead near Macon, Ga., of his grandfather, Peter; P. O., Tobesofkee.
    (a) Charles F., bookkeeper in Tampa, Fla.
    (b) J. Dudley, of Tobesofkee, Ga.
    (c) Peter W., Jr., druggist in Tallahassee, Fla.
  Peter W., Sr., married, second, Lora Wimberly; no issue.
  (3) Ellen Eliza, married, 1872, Jno. W. Huff (d. 1882), and now lives on the old Huff place near Tobesofkee, Ga. Issue:
    (a) Jno. W., Jr., married Evelyn Locke (d. 1901); issue: (a) Ellen, (b) Evelyn.
    (b) Fanny, married, 1901, W. G. Middlebrooks, a merchant in Macon, Ga.
    (c) Rosa.
  (4) Ida, married, 1870, Joseph B. Pound of Atlanta; issue:
    (a) Laura, married, 1892, Chas. Bartleson, a wholesale merchant of Jacksonville, Fla.
    (b) Norah, married Dr. Walter B. Holmes, a druggist of Wadley, Ga.
    (c) Susie, married, 1897, Jno. W. Price of Brunswick, Ga.; issue: Joseph Linwood.
    (d) Hanan J., married, 1900, Katy Jansen.
    (e) Fleeta, married, 1898, Charles Brown (d. 1899); issue: Charles.
    (f) Abner Joseph; (g) May; (h) Lurline; (i) an infant.
III. SARAH ANN (b. Sept. 19th, 1824, d. July 31st, 1853), mar-

ried, first wife, April 30th, 1843, Rev. James Lawrence King
(b. 1818, d. 1901), a distinguished Divine in the Presbyterian
church; issue:
(1) Eudora Ann (b. March 21st, 1845, d. May 28th, 1845).
(2) Horatio Leavitt (b. March 12th, 1846), married Nov.
22d, 1876, M. Josephine, daughter of Collins and Mary A.
(Ash) Lankford of Quitman, Wood county, Texas. Mr.
Lankford was a veteran of the Mexican and Confederate
wars. Issue:
(a) Angus Dallas (b. Sept. 15th, 1877, d. March 27th,
1881).
(b) Lawrence Collins (b. June 17th, 1880).
(c) Horatio Lankford (b. Oct. 11th, 1883).
(d) George Edward (b. Jan. 30th, 1886).
(e) Jessie Eugenia (b. Sept. 11th, 1888, d. Dec. 15th,
1889).
Mr. H. L. King is now a prominent lawyer in Atlanta.
(3) Maria Eugenia (b. Dec. 24th, 1847, d. Jan. 31st, 1873).
(4) John Angus (b. Nov. 24th, 1849, d. Nov. 24th, 1877).
(5) George E. (b. Nov. 3d, 1851), head of the large house,
King Hardware Co., Atlanta, Ga., and resides at Inman
Park, Atlanta; married, Oct. 21st, 1874, Ida, daughter of
Col. Jas. P. Simmons of Norcross, Ga. Issue:
(a) Jessie Eugenia (b. 1876), died young.
(b) Lucile (b. Nov. 24th, 1877), married Oct. 21st, 1896,
Irvin Summerfield Thomas; issue: Lucile Marcia (b.
May 10th, 1899).
(c) Lillian Elline (b. Oct. 23d, 1879), married Oct. 8th,
1902, Dr. Joseph Nisbet LeConte.
(d) Christine Valeria (b. Dec. 16th, 1882).
(e) Annie E. (b. June 13th, 1884, d. Aug. 10th, 1886).
(f) George E., Jr. (b. Sept. 22d, 1886).
(g) James Simmons (b. Sept. 23d, 1888), died young.
(h) Ida Ellen (b. Dec. 31st, 1889).
(i) Ruth Nelson (b. July 22d, 1892).
(j) Mary Eliza (b. Oct. 5th, 1894).
(k) Louise (b. Aug. 23d, 1896).
(6) Charles Lawrence (b. July 12th, 1853, d. Aug. 20th,
1853).
Rev. James Lawrence King married, March 2d, 1865, Martha
A. Anderson, and had Jas. L., Jr.; Clyde L., Mrs. Sam'l Farris of
La Fayette, Ga.; Mrs. Wesley Belyeu, and Mrs. Thomas Miller of
Atlanta, Ga.
IV. THOMAS (b. May 4th, 1826, d. 1877), married, first, 1846,
Mary Antonette (d. 1874), daughter of Frank and Martha

(Moody) Stubbs of Putnam county, Georgia; no issue. Married, second, 1875, Nettie Cowart; issue: Thos. Peter (b. Dec. 25th, 1875), married Jan. 21st, 1900; Minnie Vinson (d. 1891), no issue. After the death of Thomas his widow married Joel Thomas Stubbs, son of Joel G. and F. E. V. (Tankersley) Stubbs; issue: Lela (b. 1883); Joel (b. 1885), and Albert (b. 1887).

V. JAMES O. (b. July 11th, 1828). Was drowned in 1841.

VI. CAPT. CHAS. FRANCIS, C. S. A. (b. June 23d, 1830, d. July, 1882, of Bright's disease, in Savannah, Ga.); went to California during the gold fever, where he was very successful. Returned and settled in Macon, Ga., in 1855. Moved to Savannah in 1865; was member of Grover, Stubbs & Stegall, Sloan, Grover & Co., and Grover, Stubbs & Co., and C. F. Stubbs & Co. Married, April, 1876, Annie Goodwin, daughter of Theodore A. and Corinthia (Morgan) Goodwin; issue:
   (1) Charles Francis, Jr. (b. March 11th, 1877, d. July, 1888, of appendicitis).
   (2) Mary Annulette (b. Aug. 8th, 1879), married April 18th, 1900, David Stewart Craven of Salem, N. J.
   (3) Sidney Goodwin (b. Jan. 13th, 1882), now a student at Yale College.

VII. ELIZA W. (b. Feb. 22d, 1832), married Col. Charles Wesley Stubbs (C. S. A.), son of James and Lucinda (Cotton) Stubbs of Jasper county, Georgia; issue:
   (1) Charles Wesley (d. 1875), married Mattie Mitchell; issue: (a) Charlie Wesley.
   (2) Thomas Florence (b. July 17th, 1852), married Nov. 29th, 1892, Anna Martin Lawton (b. 1864,) of Buford District, S. C. They live at Inman Park, Atlanta, Ga. Issue:
      (a) Joseph Mauer (b. Sept. 29th, 1884, d. young).
      (b) Florence Eliza (b. Nov. 1st, 1886).
      (c) Carrie Martin (b. June 21st, 1888).
   (3) John W., married Gracie Carlos of Bibb county, Georgia, and is with King Hardware Co., Atlanta. No issue.
   (4) Annie Lou, married Wm. F. Holmes of Macon, Ga.; issue: (a) James Wesley, (b) Mary Ellas.

VIII. LAURA CATHERINE (b. March 9th, 1835), married Thos. Artope of Macon, Ga.; issue

(a) Leila.
(b) James, died young.
(c) Thomas Edward, married Bessie Goodwyn; issue: (a) Leila Blanche, (*b*) Minnie Goodwyn.
(d) Julia May, married 1891, Archie Reid; issue: (*a*) Laura Artope, (*b*) Edward Johnson, (*c*) Inez, (*d*) John Silon, (*e*) Henry Lamar.

IX. ELLEN M. (b. Jan. 1st, 1839), married James, son of James and Lucinda (Cotton) Stubbs of Jasper county, Georgia. No issue.

X. COL. JOHN MILTON, C. S. A. (b. Aug. 4th, 1838), a prominent lawyer and fruit grower of Dublin, Ga.; married three times. First wife, Ella Tucker; issue:
(1) Nathan T., of Fort Worth, Texas.
(2) Lucius Quintius of Dublin, Ga., representative in State Legislature; married Tallulah Ramsey of Dublin; issue: (a) Clara, (b) John.
(3) Ethel, married Harris McCall Stanley, editor of Dublin Courier; issue: (a) Lytten M., (b) Maude, (c) Harry Tucker, (d) Jno. L.
(4) Maud, married Wm. Pritchett, a merchant of Dublin, and has issue, Ethel.
Col. John M. married, second, Tallulah Johnson, daughter of Gov. Herchel V. Johnson of Georgia, and third, —— Lowe, a daughter of Gov. Lowe of Maryland. No issue by either.

XI. MARY JULIA (b. May 27th, 1843), married Joseph Bowles. Issue, Joseph.

XII. MARTHA T. (b. July 18th, 1845, d. ——), married first, Wm. Wheaton (d.) of Griffin, Ga.; issue: (1) Annie, (2) William, (3) Robert. Married, second, Mr. Trammell (d.); no issue.

XIII. ALONZO TAYLOR (b. Oct. 25th, 1848, d. young).

XIV. ROBT. H. (b. Sept. 21st, 1841, d. 1843).

## DESCENDANTS OF BARADALL PALMER AND ELIZA (HAMMOND) STUBBS.

I. SARAH CAROLINE (b. 1823, d. 1894), married 1841, Robt. W. Jemison; issue:
  (1) Henry Baradall (b. 1843, d. 1859).
  (2) Edwin Francis (b. 1845), killed at Malvern Hill (C. S. A.), July 2d, 1862.
  (3) Owen Fort (b. 1847), married Mary ——————— (d. 1902), and lives in New York; no issue.
  (4) Robt. W. (b. 1849), married, first, Kate Boifeuillat (d. 1886) ; issue:
    (a) Mamie, married July 18th, 1900, Percy Chestney of Macon, Ga.
    (b) Sarah, married Sept. 19th, 1897, Wm. Myers; issue: Robert Loring (b. Sept., 1898).
    (c) John Boifeuillat; (d) Henry, died young; (e) Annie Kate; (f) Richard.
  Robt. W. married, second, Lannie Holt Holmes; issue:
    (g) Roberta.

II. MARIA (b. Aug. 29th, 1825), married Rev. Wm. Flinn of Presbyterian Church. She died in 1853 in Demopolis, Ala., and is buried there. Issue:
  (1) Mary Owen, died young.
  (2) Sarah Jemison, married Konrad Fuhri, a professor in Normal School at Girardeau, Mo.; issue: William.
  (3) William, died young.

III. MARTHA ANN (b. May 23d, 1828), married, first, Nov. 14th, 1855, Rev. Arthur Small, pastor of Presbyterian Church in Selma, Ala. He was killed April 3d, 1865, while defending Selma against the invasion of the Northern Army, and is buried in the city cemetery. No issue. She married, second, Aug. 2d, 1867, Chancellor Smith Graham (d.) of Tuskegee, Ala.; no issue.

IV. CAPT. FRANK PETER, C. S. A. (b. Sept. 16th, 1830), prominent lawyer and planter of Monroe, La.; married, first, Jan. 9th, 1855, Margaret Linton (b. 1837, d. Nov. 4th, 1855) ; issue:
  (1) Linton W., civil engineer (b. Oct. 4th, 1855), married first, April 4th, 1882, Josephine Sloan Budd (d. 1896) of Monticello, Fla.; issue:
    (a) Margaret Josephine (b. Aug. 16th, 1886).
    (b) Bessie Gordon (b. Nov. 14th, 1891).

Married, second, Feb. 7th, 1900, Helen Chase Jones, daughter of Joseph and Josephine (Klein) Jones of Shreveport, La.

CAPT. FRANK married, second, Feb. 11th, 1858, Georgia Anna Tucker of Georgia (d. Aug. 1895); issue:

(2) Francis Baradall (b. Dec. 29th, 1858, d. Jan. 10th, 1859).

(3) Eliza Hammond (b. June 2d, 1860).

(4) Anna Virginia (b. July 11th, 1861, d. June 20th, 1862).

(5) Eugenia Tucker (b. April 4th, 1863), married April 28th, 1887, Dr. Robt. Layton (d. Jan. 4th, 1892), a prominent physician of Monroe, La.; issue:

    (a) Margaret (b. 1888).

    (b) Georgette (b. 1890).

    (c) Robert (b. 1892).

(6) Margaret Linton (b. Aug. 2d, 1865, d. June 3d, 1872).

(7) Ella Tucker (b. Nov. 4th, 1866, d. Dec. 3d, 1868).

(8) Frank (b. July 25th, 1868, d. Aug. 31st, 1869).

(9) Georgia Tucker (b. Sept. 6th, 1870), married April 19th, 1893, Victor Cameron Barringer of San Antonio, Texas; issue:

    (a) Francis Stubbs.

    (b) Victor Cameron, Jr.

(10) Major Frank Peter (b. May 4th, 1872), of Second Louisiana Volunteers in Spanish War; married May, 1898, Emily Richards of Georgetown, Ky.; issue: Frank Peter (b. Nov. 4th, 1900). Major Frank is a member of the law firm Stubbs & Russell, Monroe, La.

(11) Baradall Palmer (b. Dec. 2d, 1873, d. Aug. 24th, 1886).

(12) Guy Palmer, superintendent of Monroe Cotton Mills (b. Jan. 14th, 1875), married Nov. 19th, 1902, India King, daughter of Judge Wm. Woodson King of San Antonio, Texas.

(13) Louise (b. Sept. 16th, 1876, d. Dec. 28th, 1896).

(14) Anna Tucker (b. Jan. 4th, 1878).

(15) Mary Church (b. June 10th, 1880, d. July 4th, 1887).

V. CATHERINE PALMER (b. Nov. 22d, 1832).

VI. JULIA ELIZA (b. Dec. 20th, 1834), married Nov. 14th, 1855, Dr. Nath. Stephens Pratt, a distinguished chemist of Atlanta, Ga.; issue:

(1) Robt. Small (d. Oct. 1857).

(2) Nathaniel Palmer (b. Aug. 1867), married Frances

Baker, chemist and naturalist of Decatur, Ga.; issue: (a) Palmer, (b) Catherine Evelyn, (c) Julia Eliza, (d) Nath. Alpheus.

(3) Henry Jemison (b. 1861, d. 1892), married Fannie Prince King, who survives him, in Rozwell, Ga.; issue: (a) Richard Henry, (b) Norman Prince, (c) Henry Jemison.

(4) Frances Lorinda, a professional nurse.

(5) Arthur William (b. 1865, d. 1901, s. p.)

(6) George Lewis (b. 1875), married Meta A. Logan of New Orleans, La.; issue: (a) Margaret Logan, (b) George Lewis.

(7) Julia Eliza, married Sherrard Kennedy; issue: (a) Frances Pratt.

VII. Louisa Eugenia (b. June 6th, 1837), married Dec. 20th, 1858, Dr. Wm. Hurt Harris; issue:

(1) Myles Green, married Anne Acklen, and lives at Delta, La.; issue: (a) Catherine Palmer, (b) Mary Graham, (c) Nancy Jenkins, (d) Myles Green.

(2) Baradall Palmer, married 1898, Laura Lewis, and lives in Brunswick, Ga.; issue: (a) Rosine, (b) Baradall Palmer.

(3) Wm. Hurt, married Clifford Myddelton, and lives at Tifton, Ga.; issue: (a) Alma, (b) Wm. Hurt, (c) Eva, (d) Augustus Myddelton.

(4) Arthur Small, married Ruth Myddleton, and lives at Valdosta, Ga.; issue: (a) Ruth Randolph, (b) Louisa Eugenia Stubbs, (c) Clifford.

(5) James, married Louise Fitzgerald, and lives at Brunswick, Ga.; issue: (a) Louisa Eugenia, (b) Ada Cook.

(6) Samuel Patterson, born 1871, died July 19th, 1893, of yellow fever in Brunswick, Ga.

(7) Eliza Hammond (b. July 5th, 1873), married Wm. Stafford Irvine of Brunswick, Ga.; issue: (a) Wm. Stafford, (b) Catherine Palmer, (c) Kenneth Baillie, (d) Eugene Harris.

(8) Eugene, died young.

(9) Robert, unmarried.

VIII. Ellen Walton (b. Aug. 1st, 1843), married April 29th, 1861, Joseph Stiles King; issue:

(1) Edwin Thomas, married Clifford Fox, and lives in Miami, Fla.; issue: (a) Edwin Bird, (b) Louise Connor, (c) Wallace, (d) Eleanor.

(2) Joseph King, died young.

(3) Ralph, married Marian Puckett, and lives on Indian River, Fla.; issue: LeRoy.

(4) Graham Walton; married Edith Carling and lives at Miami, Fla.

(5) Margaret Esther, married Wm. Bea Da, and lives in Atlanta, Ga.; issue: Gertrude.

(6) Richard Stubbs, lives in Florida.

(7) Dwight Adams, lives in Florida.

IX. WILLIAM BARADALL (b. June 15th, 1840), Colonel C. S. A. Died of camp fever, at Midway, Ga., July 17th, 1864.

X. EMMA CLINTON (b. March 15th, 1846), married May 15th, 1867, Charles Pratt; issue:

(1) James Pryor, died young.

(2) Eliza Richard (b. 1871).

(3) Willie Stubbs (b. 1873).

(4) Emma Clinton (b. 1880).

(5) Ellen Palmer (b. 1884).

(6) Eugene C. (b. 1889).

XI. RICHARD NICHOLLS (b. May 23d, 1849). Died in Savannah, Ga., of yellow fever, Nov. 15th, 1871; unmarried. "A beautiful life cut off in midst of great promise of usefulness and 'success."

## OTHER BRANCHES OF THE FAMILY.

There is a family of Stubbses, widely scattered through the South, that are the descendants of a George Stubbs who married Sarah Osprey. This George is said to have been the son of James Stubbs and had a brother Thomas, well known to the older members of the family, and another brother, Samuel, of whom nothing is known.

George Stubbs lived and died at Cuthbert, Ga. He had a first cousin by name of Thos. Stubbs. The above, obtained from living members of the family, may be correct. It is possible for George and Samuel to be sons of James and Mary Eliza (Scott) Stubbs, ten of whose children have already been given, among them a son of Thomas. James had a brother, Peter, who had also a son Thomas.

This may be the origin of this family, but it is uncertain and it is therefore deemed prudent to place this branch alone until future investigation shall transfer it to its proper place.

### *Descendants of George Stubbs of Cuthbert, Ga., and His Wife, Sarah Osprey.*

I. WILLIAM OSPREY, (b. *circa*, 1820, d.), married, first, Martha McLendon, and had:

> (1) Geo. W., of Hamilton, Tex. He lost an eye in the C. S. A. Married Miss Wright of Alabama, and have several children.
>
> Married, second, Mary Mandeville; issue:
>
> (2) Charles, of Thomas county, Georgia; married Miss Maitland of Cuthburt, Ga., and has several children.
>
> (3) Rev. Harrison, M. E. Church South (d.), married Jeannie Proctor and left several children.

II. JAMES (b. circa 1822, d. circa 1845), married Miss Grier, and had Samuel. His widow married, second, Thomas Glover.

III. MATHEW (b. circa 1824), married Elizabeth Bingham; issue:

> (1) Eugenia, married Wayne Anderson, Cortes P. O., Matagorda county, Texas.
>
> (2) Louise, married E. M. Wallace of Cuero, Dewitt county, Texas.

(3) Winnie, married J. H. McCrocklin of Kendalia, Kendall county, Texas.

(4) Rufus, died young; (5) Ada, died young; (6) William, died young.

(7) Della, married W. S. Gossett, Troup, Texas.

(8) Estelle, died young.

(9) Thomas M., married Nobia Harrington, Blanco, Texas.

IV. LEMUEEL, married Winnie Bingham; issue:

(1) Ida, married Isaac Bagby of Austin, Texas.

(2) Dora, married Wm. Page.

(3) Benjamin J., married Ophelia Palmer of Johnson City, Blanco county, Texas.

(4) Lemuel G., married ————, Fredericksburg, Texas.

(5) Nathaniel T., married Julia Johnson of Johnson City, Texas.

(6) Albert L., married, first, Ophelia Grier, Llano, Texas; second, Temperance Bingham; has issue.

(7) Clara, of Elgin, Texas.

(8) Ada, married Samuel Brown of Georgetown, Texas.

(9) Oscar A., principal of Fredericksburg High School, Fredericksburg, Texas.

(10) James B., of Blanco, Texas.

(11) Alma, of Blanco, Texas.

V. THOMAS (b. June 1st, 1828, d. Feb. 6th, 1884), of Athens, Ala.; married Rebecca Dozier of Oglethorpe county, Georgia; issue:

(1) Eudora, married Dr. J. B. Sawyer (d. 1900) of Fayetteville, Tenn., and moved to Galveston, Texas; issue:

(a) Mary (d. 1900), married C. W. Howth.

(b) Ossapha Burgess, of Beaumont, Texas.

(c) Thos. Lyle of Galveston, Texas, married ——.

In the fearful storm at Galveston in September, 1900, Dr. Sawyer and his lovely daughter, recently married, were killed.

(2) Ossapha Ophelia, married, first, James Rutland of Alabama, and had a daughter, Eudora, who married E. J. Blackwood of Birmingham, Ala. Married, second, Wm. Henderson Smith of Franklin, Tenn.

Mrs. Rebecca Dozier Stubbs lives with her daughter, Mrs. Smith, of Tennessee.

VI. ELLA, married Felix Grier; issue:

(1) Elizabeth, married Alfred Kelsaw.

(2) Adran, married Benj. Brigham of Joonah, Texas.

(3) Laura, married Edward Lindeman of Blanco, Texas.
(4) Mildred, married ———.
(5) Matilda, married Needham Smith.

VII. MARIA, married Eli Grier of Blanco, Texas; issue:
   (1) Jackson Stubbs, married, first, Mary Hoges; second, Martha Caldwell.
   (2) Bethia, married Benjamin Cage of Blanco, Texas.

VIII. CAROLINE, married Thomas Borland of Dale county, Alabama, and had among others, Hampton Borland, Pinckard, Dale county, Alabama.

IX. BASHABA (d.), married Bynum Page (d); issue: Louise, died young.

### Descendants of a Thomas Stubbs.

It is probable, says Rev. Geo. G. Smith of Georgia, that THOMAS (b. circa 1770) is a son of Benjamin of the Revolution, to whom was issued a land warrant for services.

Thomas, it seems, married twice; the first time to Miss Jones, who drowned herself. The issue by the first marriage were the following, though some of the descendants of Thomas assert that he had twelve children by his first wife—which is probable:
   (1) Nancy.
   (2) Millie, married Gilmore, and has a son, Stubbs Gilmore, living in Washington county, Georgia.
   (3) Mary.
   (4) Margaret.
   (5) Ann.
   (6) Benjamin.
   (7) Amariah Biggs.
   (8) Richard, died young.
Thomas settled first in Washington county and moved when Benjamin was a boy to Wilkinson county, Georgia. After death of first wife he moved to Harris county, Georgia, where he died at an advanced age. He married, second, Widow Betsy Wadsworth, *nee* Tate, the niece of Nathaniel Tate, and had seven children:
   (9) Wm. Franklin (b. 1815, d. 1829) in Henry county, Georgia. See further on for issue.
   (10) Richard, died young.
   (11) Elvira, married Bolton.
   (12) Frutilla, married a doctor near Atlanta, Ga.

(13) Ann, married Bolton, after death of sister.
(14) A daughter.
(15) A daughter.
(6) Benjamin, above (b. circa 1797), married Fannie Parker; issue:
  (a) Robt. Lawrence (b. 1823, d. March 13th, 1865), married Martha Ann Bush. She married, second, Pittman. Issue of Robt. Lawrence:
    (a) Emma, married, first, Lester; and second, Morris.
    (b) Wm. B., member of law firm of Gynilliat & Stubbs of Savannah, Ga.; married Miss Carson.
    (c) Bettie F., married W. K. Wilkinson.
    (d) Robt. Emmett of Abbeville, Ga. (b. Sept. 4th, 1863), married Feb. 1890, Alice Fuller (d. 1901); issue: (1) Emma Lou, b. 1893; (2) Martha Grace, b. 1896; (3) Alice Eone, b. 1898; (4) Elizabeth Fuller, b. 1901.
  (b) Eliza (b. 1825, d. 1860), married Stevens; issue:
    (a) James, married Brewer.
    (b) Frances, married Carr.
    (c) Martha, unmarried.
    (d) Babbie, unmarried.
    (e) Robert, married Harrell.
    (f) Thomas, married DeSaw.
    (g) ——, married Collins.
  (c) Hannah (b. 1823), still living at Toombsboro, Ga., and has furnished much family data; married, first, Thos. Underwood; second, Augustus Craft; issue:
    (a) Thomas Underwood.
    (b) Susannah Underwood.
    (c) Wm. Craft.
    (d) Fannie Craft.
  (d) Falby (b. 1829), married Waters and died s. p.
  (e) Seaborn Jones (b. 1827, d. 1870), married, first, Selina Brannon (d. 1856); married, second, 1857, Elizabeth Ivy (b. 1838). Issue by first wife:
    (a) Benjamin.
    (b) Tallulah.
Issue by second wife:
    (c) Eliza Sarah, died young.
    (d) Clifford Lillian (b. 1860), married, first, Newman Smith; second, M. E. Wheeler.
    (e) Ferney Bartow, of Macon, Ga. (b. Nov., 1861) married Rosa Lee Bussey; issue: (1) Claude, b. Aug. 11th, 1887; (2) Bessie, b. Sept. 27th, 1889; (3) Maude, b. March, 1893; (4) Joseph, b. Sept., 1895.

(*f*) Sidney Johnson (b. Oct. 11th, 1863), married Sept. 18th, 1895, Mary Eliza Clements; issue: (1) Sidney, (2) Francis Seaborn.

(*g*) Robt. Lee of Wilkinson county, Georgia (b. 1868), married Cornelia Spencer; issue: (1) Clyde, (2) Leo, (3) Hannah, (4) Herbert, (5) Ruth.

(*h*) Ivy Claudius of Mitchell county, Georgia (b. 1870), married Cornelia Lord; issue: (1) Cora, (2) Evelina, (3) Julian, (4) Clifford.

Mr. S. J. Stubbs and brother owned Bibb Land & Lumber Co. at Cox, Ga., and afterwards the Williams Co. at Eastman, Ga. Mr. S. J. Stubbs owns a beautiful home in Vineville, near Macon, Ga.

(f) Nancy, married Hatcher.

(g) Amariah, died s. p. 15 years old.

(h) Thomas, died young.

(7) Amariah Biggs (b. Aug. 10th, 1806), the seventh child of Thomas and —— (Jones) Stubbs, was named for the minister who baptized his mother. He was a Baptist preacher and married Mary A. Peacock (b. 1810, d. 1893), of Muscogee county, Georgia, and moved to Dale county, Alabama, where he died Aug. 31st, 1873. Issue:

(1) Jonathan T. (b. May 3d, 1831), died young.

(2) Sarah A. (b. Jan. 25th, 1833), married Daniel McLean; issue: (a) Daniel, (b) Laurantine.

(3) James W. (b. June 9th, 1835, d. C. S. A.), a Baptist preacher, married Eliza Chaney; issue: Theodora.

(4) Mary R. (b. May 20th, 1838, d. Oct. 24th, 1880), married, first, John Jackson (d. C. S. A.); issue: Jessie A. and Mary E. Married, second, J. A. Dixon (d.); issue: Martha Susan.

(5) Martha M. (b. June 30th, 1840), married B. F. Jackson, killed in C. S. A. Issue: James T.

(6) Elizabeth K. (b. April 23d, 1843), married J. R. Brown; issue: Wm. Arnold.

(7) Benjamin J. (b. April 23d, 1843), died in C. S. A.

(8) Nancy A. (b. May 9th, 1845), married P. W. Bailey; issue: (a) Elizabeth, (b) Missouri, (c) Jennie, (d) Henry.

(9) Missouri E. (b. Feb. 18th, 1848), married Wm. L. Faust (d. 1885); issue: (a) Mary L., (b) Martha E., (e) Franklin G., (d) Wm. L., (e) Amariah Biggs, (f) Daniel W. All living and married.

(10) Jno. Samuel (b. June 16th, 1850), married Ellen Brown; issue: (a) Mary E., (b) Nancy A.

(11) Amariah Biggs, Jr., of Arguta P. O., Dale county, Alabama (b. May 27th, 1852); married Oct. 19th, 1876, Mary Ann Tillman; issue: (a) Jno. Samuel, b. Dec. 5th, 1877; (b) James Robt., b. Aug. 2d, 1880; (c) Amariah Biggs, b. Feb. 3d, 1882; (d) Wm. Faust, b. Jan. 25th, 1885; (e) Mary Ann, b. Dec. 8th, 1887; (f) Stephen Coleman, b. Oct. 14th, 1889. All living and none married.

Wm. Franklin, the oldest child of Thomas by his second wife, Betsy Wadsworth, *nee* Tate, was born in 1815 and died in 1879, in Henry county, Georgia, near McDonough; married, 1850, Sarah Caroline Worrell (d. 1883); issue:

(1) Lavinia L., married 1872, Dr. Thos. Lunda Jenkins of Chipley, Ga.; issue: Ira Lunda (b. 1872, d. 1899), a graduate of Oxford College and a young man of fine promise.

(2) Sarah Franklyn, married A. C. Cantrell.

(3) Lula, unmarried.

(4) W. W., married Mary Swaner; issue: three children, and live in Texas.

(5) Arthur Fort, married Lucy Hahn of New Orleans, La., and has one child.

(6) R. G., a traveling salesman.

*Descendants of John and Anna (Wallace) Stubbs of Georgia, but Originally from North Carolina.*

John Stubbs (b. circa 1778-80) moved from North Carolina near the coast on the Dismal Swamp, and settled in Wilkes county, Georgia, about 1800. About one year later he moved to Washington county, Georgia, where he died. He married Anna Wallace in North Carolina (d. 1847), who had half-brothers and sisters by name of Everett; her mother marrying first an Everett and second a Wallace. Hardy Everett (d. 1854), was a half-brother. The above facts gleaned from the family records suggest descent of John from Richard Stubbs of Bath county, North Carolina, who moved from Virginia about 1703. Issue of John and Anna (Wallace) Stubbs.

I. GABRIEL WALLACE (b. 1807, d. 1880), married 1828, Grace N. Collins (b. 1812, died in Sandersville, Ga., March, 1902); issue:

(1)  Archibald McNeal, C. S. A. (b. Oct. 3d, 1833), married
1854, Mrs. Caroline A. Everett (d. 1886), of Tenille, Ga.
Issue:
(a)  Thomas A., married Belle Lowe of Wellborn, Fla.,
and has three children.
(b)  Brooks P., married ―― May and lives in Jackson-
ville, Fla., and has three children.
(c)  Gabriella Floried, married, first, Benj. O. Smith (d.
1886); married, second, Dr. H. W. Orr, and has four
children.
(d)  Grace Floried, married Gordon W. Smith, and has
six children.
(e)  John G. (b. 1860), unmarried.
(f)  Minnie LeOlean, married Jno. A. Smith of Bullock
county, Georgia, and has three children.
(2)  Jasper Newton, C. S. A., badly wounded (b. 1835),
married, 1885, Miss Peddy of Adrian, Ga.  His postoffice
address is Harrison, Ga.  Issue: two children.
(3)  Mollie (d. 1880), married, 1856, A. W. Stewart; issue:
eight children.
(4)  Edwin Everett, C. S. A. (d.), married Miss Gray (d.),
and had one child.  All now dead.
(5)  Frank Marion of Augusta, Ga. (b. 1845), married, first,
Miss Parker (d.), and second, Miss Shaly (d. 1902).  No
issue.
(6)  Margaret, married, 1865, Misell G. Wood, Jr. (d.) of
Sandersville, Ga., and has four children.
(7)  Emma, married, 1860, Daniel Ainsworth (d.) of Sandersville, Ga., and has two children.
(8)  Martha, married Wm. Haines Renfro of Cartersville,
Ga., and has three children.
(9)  Sarah, married Charles M. Joyner of Rome, Ga., and
has six children.

II. Polly, born in North Carolina, died in Texas, married, in
1820, Reuben Manning, and moved, first, to Florida, and then to
Texas in 1845, and has descendants in Limestone county, Texas.

III. Eliza, married Edward Armstrong of Washington, Ga.,
and have only grandchildren living.

IV. Emma, married Edmond May and died s. p.

## PERSONAL CHAPTER.

It will not, I trust, be deemed inappropriate to insert here a more extended record of those who are near and dear to the writer.

It was always a pleasant duty to give proper respect, obedience and affection to my devoted parents when they were alive, and now after death it is with peculiar pride that we chronicle their many virtues.

In the old graveyard at Valley Front, a monument of purest marble bears the following inscription:

"OUR MOTHER,

"Ann Walker Carter Stubbs, wife of Jefferson W. Stubbs, Esq., eldest daughter of Capt. James Baytop and Lucy Taliaferro Catlett, his wife, of Springfield, in the county of Gloucester, the ancient seat of the family and place of her nativity. She died on the 22d September, 1894, in the 78th year of her age and the 60th of her marriage. She was of great and exemplary piety and charity and in every relation of life, whether considered as a Christian, a wife, a mother, a mistress, a neighbor or a friend, she was equalled by few and excelled by none.

"Death came peacefully and with gentle step and with tender touch, framed a lullaby fit for a Christian's rest."

This monument was erected by her children and their modest tribute to her exalted worth is more than corroborated by the many eulogiums spoken by her neighbors, friends and acquaintances. From a large number only extracts from two will be given. The first is by the Rev. James C. Martin, once her pastor, who officiated at her golden wedding, and a distinguished minister in the Virginia Methodist Conference. He, too, has since gone to reap his reward.

"Her marriage was blessed with a large family of children, a number of whom preceded her to the better land. * * * Her boys on earth are the Hon. James N. Stubbs, state senator; Prof. Thos. Jefferson Stubbs of William and Mary College, and Prof. William C. Stubbs of the Louisiana State University. * * * The writer of these lines was honored with a chief place at their golden wedding, which occurred at Valley Front about ten years ago. Never was there a more beautiful and appropriate hour expressive of a long and happy union of two loving hearts * *

\*   She was a friend to the poor; the widow and orphan, the sick
and the suffering knew the tone of her voice, the kindness of her
hands, and rise up to call her blessed.   \*   \*   \*   If children have
ever had a truer, sweeter, tenderer, nobler Christian mother, I
have failed to see her.   If husband has ever had a finer type of
all that constitutes a real helpmeet, I have never known her.   If
church and community have cause to mourn the loss of one of
their chief treasures, then many eyes were moist with tears when
God took this venerable woman to Himself.   Mourners white
and colored, in great numbers, gathered at Valley Front on the
day of her burial.   Rev. J. D. Hank, her pastor, assisted by the
Rev. Wm. E. Wiatt of the Baptist church—the Rev. Wm. B.
Lee of the Episcopal church, performed the funeral services at
Valley Front, and then the mortal remains were laid to rest in the
graveyard there, where have slept the precious dust of the house
of Stubbs for an hundred years."

The second extract is from the pen of Prof. Alexander Hogg
of Fort Worth, Texas, our first male teacher:

"It is a pardonable if a proud recollection of the writer that her
boys were among his first pupils.

"The greatest amount of care for the sick and distressed was
during the late war, when the troops at Yorktown were stricken,
under the terrible results of camp life.   Gloucester county extended a welcome to these sufferers, and 'Valley Front' cared for over
fifty at a time, and thus for months its charity never failed.

"But yesterday, the writer listened to an essay in which the
virtues of the Spartan women were extolled.   Spartan women!
Roman mothers!!   Virginia has furnished as great examples of
womanly virtue, Christian character and patriotic devotion as the
world ever saw.

"She gave the service of her three sons to the Confederate
cause.

"The funeral was the largest ever seen in the county.   There
was about this a fitness and a tenderness that must be mentioned
here that will not soon be forgotten by those who witnessed the
same.   Her remains were borne to their last resting place, just
over the ravine, in full view of the house—a bright spot—by her
sons, her grandsons, her nephews and her cousins.   The home at
Valley Front will be gloomy this Christmas.   The neighbors and
friends who are accustomed annually to meet there will miss the
bright cheer and large hospitality of this household—this homestead that has been occupied by the same family descendants
through several generations.

"Not least among those who will sigh are the old family servants. Few people understand the close and confiding relations that existed between there and their old owners. \* \* \*

"But out of all these losses and the exceeding sorrow of the household, a bright gleam—a radiant assurance comes to us, that society, the church, the state and mankind have been helped, have been infinitely blessed, through the noble character, the Christian life and the patriotic devotion of Mrs. Jefferson W. Stubbs."

Side by side with our mother lies our father, Jefferson W. Stubbs, who followed her to the grave a few years later.

The Richmond *Christian Advocate* says:

"He had attained his eighty-sixth year and had been for more than sixty years recording steward of Gloucester Circuit, witnessing in that long period as many as six rearrangements of the territory known by that name as a pastoral charge.

"After a long and faithful service, active, intelligent and useful, 'he sleeps well,' his mortal part resting beside the dust of his wife, who was removed from his home a few years since and placed amidst the graves of other loved ones of his own and past generations.

"The place on which he lived so long, being there born and dying there, had been inherited from his father and has been in the possession of the Stubbs family for more than a hundred years. Their title is traced directly to the grant from the British crown."

Tributes of respect were paid to his memory by the stewards of the M. E. Church, South, of which he was a member for nearly sixty years; by the Gloucester Charity School, of which he was for fifty years president, and by the bar and people of Gloucester county, where he was the presiding justice for many years. The following are extracts from resolutions of the Gloucester Charity School:

"WHEREAS, The relations as chief officer and fellow associate of this corporation held for a series of more than four decades, render it proper that we should place upon record our high appreciation of his valuable services as an officer and member, and his merits as a citizen; therefore,

"*Resolved*, That his memory as a man and as a fellow member, as president of this corporation, and as a Christian gentleman is precious to us all, and will remain unclouded as the years roll on.

"That for his keen perception of right and wrong, his unswerving fidelity to duty, his wise counsels, his discriminating judgment, and prudent forethought, his commendable conservatism, his fervid sympathy for the needy, the Gloucester Charity School and the community have sustained a great loss.

"That no token of affection can be too profuse, no mark of respect too emphatic, no rendition of honor too conspicuous for one whose virtues were so eminent and whose memory is so deeply enshrined in the affections of his associates.

"WM. F. HOGG,
"CHAS. CATLETT,
"THOS. S. TALIAFERRO,
*"Committee."*

At a meeting of the bar and people of Gloucester county to take appropriate action with reference to the death of Jefferson W. Stubbs, General William B. Taliaferro was made chairman and Maryus Jones secretary, and the following resolutions were adopted:

*"Resolved* (1), That we have heard with profound sorrow of the death of Mr. Jeff. W. Stubbs, for many years the presiding justice of the county of Gloucester, as organized before the adoption of the present constitution of the state.

*"Resolved* (2), That Mr. Stubbs had been prominent in all business and religious affairs of the county for many years, and although his age and infirm health had for some years prevented him from active participation in the affairs of life, we feel that a prominent landmark is missing from the county and the church.

*"Resolved* (3), That the portrait of Mr. Stubbs now hanging in the courthouse be draped in mourning for thirty days.

*"Resolved* (4), That these resolutions be spreads on the records of the county court of Gloucester county," etc.

Appropriate remarks were made by Wm. Ap. W. Jones, Maryus Jones, Rev. Wm. E. Wiatt, R. McCandlish, T. G. Jones, Capt. R. M. Page, James L. Stubbs, Jno. B. Donovan, H. R. Corr, and General Wm. B. Taliaferro.

The three sons mentioned in the above notice are:

(1) MAJOR JAMES NEW STUBBS of "Church Hill," Gloucester county, Virginia; a lawyer of large practice. Educated at William and Mary College, and studied law under Judge Jno. W. Brockenborough, Lexington, Va., in 1860-61. After the war he completed his law course at the University of Virginia. Entered the Confederate States Army in 1861, as a member of the "Gloucester" artilley (Red Shirts). Was detailed for duty in the "Signal Corps" early in the war, in which service he remained, rising to the rank of "Major." He accompanied General Jno. Bankhead Magruder to Texas in 1862, and remained with him until the close of the war. He rendered valuable service in the capture of the Harriet Lane off Galveston. After the war he resumed his law studies and began practice in 1866. He was elected

member of House of Delegates in 1869, and since that time has served almost continuously either as a delegate or State Senator. He is vice-president of the Board of Visitors of William and Mary College and until recently was president of the Board of Control of the Blind and Deaf and Dumb Asylum at Staunton, Virginia. Has been State Commander of the Confederate Veterans of Virginia and was largely instrumental in the erection of the handsome monument to the Confederate dead at Gloucester Court House. He is a member of Botetourt Lodge No. 7 of Free and Accepted Masons. He married in 1866, Eliza Medlicott, daughter of Joseph and Hester (Shackelford) Medlicott, and a granddaughter of Wm. and Eliza (Munson) Shackelford of Salem, Gloucester county, Virginia.

(2) PROF. THOS. JEFFERSON STUBBS is an A. M. graduate of William and Mary College, and Ph. D. of Arkansas College, Arkansas, in which institution he was a professor for many years. In 1877 and 1879 was a representative in the General Assembly of Arkansas. He was a gallant member, during the entire war, of Co. A, 34th Va. Infantry, Wise's Brigade, a company of heavy artillery at the beginning of the war and known as the "Red Shirts." He is now and has been since 1888, Professor of Mathematics in William and Mary College, Williamsburg, Va. He is a Mason and an elder in the Presbyterian church. He married, 1869, Mary Mercer Cosnahan of Williamsburg, Va., daughter of Capt. Joseph B. Cosnahan (C. S. A.) and Louisa Mercer Waller, daughter of Dr. Robt. Page Waller and Julia Weeden Mercer. Capt. Cosnahan was an attorney-at-law, a native of South Carolina and "an accomplished gentleman, a sincere friend and a faithful soldier." Prof. Stubbs' children were all born in Arkansas.

(3) "DR. WILLIAM CARTER STUBBS, after being trained for college with his two brothers by the best private tutors, entered William and Mary College in 1860. This college suspending exercises in 1861, his college curiculum was completed by graduation at Randolph Macon in 1862. In September he entered a company of "Partisan Rangers," commanded by Capt. Thos. C. Clopton. This company became later Co. D, 24th Va. Cavalry, with which he served as an officer throughout the war, surrendering at Appomattox Court House in April, 1865. In October, 1865, he resumed his studies at the University with his two brothers, mentioned above, and remained until graduation. While at the University of Virginia he was a competitor for the Mathematical medal, nobly but unsuccessfully contending with Gaetano Lanza, now professor of applied mathematics in the School of

Technology, Boston, Mass.  In 1869 he accepted a professorship
in East Alabama College, and in 1872 was made professor of
chemistry in Alabama Agricultural and Mechanical College, Auburn, Ala.  In 1878 was made state chemist of Alabama.  In
1885 was called to Louisiana to take charge of Louisiana Sugar
Experiment Station, established by the sugar planters of this
state.  He was soon appointed professor of agriculture in Louisiana State University and director of State Experiment Station
at Baton Rouge.  In 1886 was made by Legislature, state chemist of Louisiana, and in 1887 director of the North Louisiana
Experiment Station at Calhoun, La.  In 1892 was empowered by
the Legislature of the state, with suitable appropriation, to con-
duct a geological survey of the state.  In the same year the Audubon Sugar School was established and placed under his direction.
From small beginnings he has witnessed with delight the evolu-
tion of agricultural teachings, until to-day few states can claim
more agencies at work in behalf of agriculture than Louisiana.
The gradually increasing appropriations made biennially by the
Legislature of the state are the best evidences of the appreciation
of the public of his laborious work.  He has published over one
hundred bulletins upon various agricultural topics and has become
an authority on Southern agriculture.  His published works on
sugar cane and the manufacture of sugar are known and appreci-
ated wherever sugar cane is grown.  He has also published several brochures on genealogy.  His residence is Audubon Park,
New Orleans.  He is a member of Camp No. 9, C. S. V., and of
General Jno. B. Gordon's staff, holding his commission as Brigadier General.  He was commissioned, in 1900, by Hon. James
Wilson, Secretary of Agriculture, to visit the Hawaiian Islands,
report upon their agricultural resources and locate an experiment
station.  His report to the Secretary was transmitted to Congress
by President McKinley and published as House Document No.
368.  He has served as state commissioner at the following expo-
sitions: Cotton States Exposition, Atlanta, Ga.; Pan-American at
Buffalo, and that at Charleston.  He has been recently appointed
commissioner for Louisiana at the Louisiana Purchase Exposition
at St. Louis for 1904.  He is a Mason, a member of Knights of
Honor, and a Democrat.  He married, in 1875, Elizabeth Saunders Blair, daughter of Henry Dickinson and Mary Louisa (Saunders) Blair, and granddaughter of Col. James E. and Mary (Watkins) Saunders of Rocky Hill, Lawrence county, Alabama.  Her
father was son of John J. and Martha (Ray) Blair of Camden, S.
C., and Mobile, Ala.  Mrs. Stubbs, aided by her grandfather, Col.
James E. Saunders, has recently published "Early Settlers of Alabama, and Notes and Genealogies," an octavo volume of over 500
pages."

## BAYTOP EXCURSUS.

THOMAS BAYTOP, merchant of Virginia, came from Staplehurst, Kent county, England, in 1679 (d. 1690) ; married Hannah ——— and had:

THOMAS (b. 1676 in England), who married ——— Alexander, daughter of Dr. David and Mary (Morgan) Alexander. Issue:

(1) ANN, married Col. Thomas Scott and was the ancestress of the Scotts, McGehees, and some of the Stubbses of the South.

(2) COL. JAMES BAYTOP of Springfield, Gloucester county, Virginia (d. 1766), tobacco inspector 1754; married Sarah Smith (believed to be) of "Purton;" issue:

(A) Capt. Thomas of the Revolution (b. 1751, d. 1812), member of Legislature, member of Vestry of Ware parish and tobacco inspector; married Sarah Booth, daughter of Geo. Booth of "Poropotank," and had issue, among others:

I. Capt. and Rev. James of the war of 1812; member of Legislature (b. 1792, d. 1860) ; married Lucy Taliaferro Catlett of "Timberneck;" issue:

(a) Thomas Charles (b. 1815, d. 1893), married, first, Sarah McLaughlin (d. 1864) ; second, Caroline Dabney (d. 1885) ; no issue.

(b) Ann Walker Carter (b. 1817, d. 1894), married Jeff. W. Stubbs of "Valley Front" and was the mother of the writer.

(c) Capt. Wm. Jones, C. S. A., killed at Seven Pines, 1862; married Rebecca Dobson, and was the father of Mrs. Col. W. W. Green of West Point, Va.

(d) Lieut. James Christopher, C. S. A. (d. 1896), married Josephine Spottswood Lewis; no issue.

(e) Lucy Helen (d. 1900), married Jno. Sinclair of "Sherwood" and has issue in Virginia and Arkansas.

(f) Martha Agnes (d. 1898), married Dr. Walker F. Jones (d. 1900) of "Sunnyside," and has issue in Virginia and Arkansas.

(g) Henrietta Ellen (d. 1902), married Col. Rufus King Fitzhugh (d. 1888) of "Walnut Woods," Ark., and has seven sons and three daughters, all in Arkansas.

(h) Rowena Matilda (d. 1873), married Robt. M. Sinclair and left issue in Virginia.

(i) Indiana W., married Charles W. Montague (d. 1888), and lives with her children in Arkansas.

(j) Margaret Eugenia, married, first, Thos. W. Banks (died C. S. A.) ; married, second, Robt. Shields, and lives with her children in Newport News, Va.

(B) Sarah, married Cornelius Livingston and has descendants living in Baltimore, Md.

(C) Capt. James of the Revolution (b. 1754, d. 1822), member of Legislature, vestry of Petsworth, member of "Order of Cincinnatus," and justice; married three times—first, Mary Cooke; second, Mrs. Elizabeth Whiting, *nee* Robinson; third, Catherine Klug Yates. Issue only by first wife. The late Col. Jno. Baytop Cary of Richmond, Va., and his brothers were descendants from this marriage.

(D) Mary, married Francis Whiting Cooke. (See Cooke pamphlet for descent.

(E) Sarah, married Philip Taliaferro of "Hockley," King and Queen county, Virginia, and was the ancestress of the Taliaferros of Gloucester county, Virginia, including the late Major General Wm. Booth Taliaferro, C. S. A.

(F) Lieut. John of the Revolution (b. 1756, d. 1821 s. p.)

### Booth Excursus.

Thomas Booth, the immigrant from Barton, Lancashire, England, where he was born in 1663. Settled on Ware River, Gloucester county, Virginia, where he died in 1736. Thomas the immigrant, was the son of "St. John, who was son of John, the son of George. George was also the father of Wm. who was the father of George, first Lord Delamere, who was father of Henry Booth, Earl of Delamere." (Macauley's History.) Thomas married Mary (d. 1723), the daughter of Mordecai Cooke of "Mordecai's Mount." Their tombs, with *arms,* are at Jarvis Farm, Gloucester county, Virginia.
They had ten children, viz:

(I.) Thomas (b. 1685, d. 1756) of Hanover; married three times: first, Ann Buckner, daughter Maj. Thomas and Sarah (Morgan) Buckner, and had:
(1) Capt. George of "Poropotank" (d. 1786), member of vestry of Petsworth, who had eight children, as follows:
(a) Thos. (d. 1804), sheriff of Gloucester; married, first, Mary Allen; second, Ann Dudley; and left numerous issue.
(b) Ann, married Stephen Field, Jr., and left issue.

(c) Sarah, married Capt. Thos. Baytop of "Springfield," and were the parents of Capt. and Rev. James Baytop, Jr., grandfather of the writer.

(d) Mary, married, first, Francis Duval, and second, Mathew Kemp, and left issue.

(e) Elizabeth, married James Wiatt and left issue.

(f) Margaret, married Nathaniel Lipscomb, and left issue.

(g) Frances, married Thomas Cooke of "Wareham." Died s. p.

(h) Catherine, married James Baytop Taliaferro, and left issue.

THOMAS married, second, Susannah Thornton, and had:

(2) Thomas of Henrico.

(3) Seth Thornton, died young.

Married, third, Lucy, daughter of Jno. and Ann (Todd) Cooke and widow of Gregory Smith, and had:

(4) John Cooke (b. 1749, d. 1773), married Ann Brown and had an only daughter. Mary Cooke (b. 1772), who married in 1793, Col. Morgan Tomkies, and left one son, John Francis Tomkies, whose descendants live in Louisiana.

(5) Mary Cooke (b. 1750, d. 1820), married Rev. Emanuel Jones and had Richard, who married Martha Throckmorton; and Lucy, who married George Wythe Booth.

(6) Mordecai Cooke, married Ann Maddox.

II. DR. GEORGE, married Frances —— (d. 1768). and had Thomas and (possibly) Wm. of Woodstock; both died s. p.

III. MARY BOOTH, married John Perrin of "Sarah's Creek."

IV. MORDECAI. merchant of Yorktown and Gloucester: married Joyce, daughter of Wm. and Ann (Lee) Armistead of "Hesse." and had George of "Bellville," who was the great-grandfather of General Wm. Booth Taliaferro of Gloucester county, Virginia, and father of George Wythe Booth, above.

V. ELIZABETH, married Rev. Pryse Davis of New Kent county, Virginia.

VI. JNO. BOOTH (b. 1705, d. 1748), commander of ship "Mermaid," died s. p.

VII. ISABEL (b. 1704, d. 1742), married Rev. Jno. Fox and left issue.

VIII. ANN (d. 1775), married, first, Thomas Reade; second, Jno. Shermer. No issue.

IX. CATHERINE, died s. p.

X. WILLIAM of Frederick county (d. 1789), married, 1750, Elizabeth Aylett, daughter Col. Wm. and Ann (Ashton) Aylett. Issue:
(1) Wm. Aylett (b. 1754, d. 1820), Colonel in Revolution, of Louisville, Ky.; married Rebecca Hite of Winchester, Va., and had fourteen children. From him are descended the Booths of Kentucky, St. Louis and Louisiana.
(2) Ann Aylett, married Samuel Beall, and had issue.
(3) Mordecai, married Clara Waller and had Capt. Benj. Waller Booth of U. S. A., and died in command of Mediterranean fleet, and buried at Gibraltar; and Wm. Lee Booth, graduate of West Point, married Ann M. Beall.

For an account of MORDECAI COOKE, the immigrant from Whitefield, county Suffolk, England, see "Cooke Pamphlet."

### BUCKNER EXCURSUS.

There appears to have been at least two immigrants by this name: JOHN, who patented lands in Gloucester soon after it was opened for settlement; and PHILIP of Stafford—presumably brothers. Philip had sons Robt. and Andrew. John is believed to have married a Miss Cooke and had Wm. of Yorktown, Thos. and John of Gloucester, and Richard of Essex, who married Elizabeth Cooke.

Of these Maj. Thomas of Gloucester married Sarah, daughter of Capt. Francis Morgan, and had issue:

(1) Thomas (d. 1755), married Mary Timson, and had issue: Baldwin Mathews, John, Mordecai, Wm., and Mary.
(2) Col. Samuel (d. 1763), married Ann ——, and had:
(a) Dorothy (b. 1730, d. 1757), married Baldwin Mathews Buckner (d. 1778).
(b) Elizabeth, married Wm. Finnie.
(c) Mary, married Rev. Chas. Mynn Thruston, the "Fighting Parson" of the Revolution.
(3) Ann, married Thomas Booth, and had George of "Poropotank," the ancestor of the writer.
The Buckners were from London, England.

## SMITH EXCURSUS.

MAJOR LAWRENCE SMITH (d. 1700), surveyor for Gloucester and York counties, Virginia. Laid out Yorktown in 1691. Patented "Severn Hall" in Gloucester county, 1662, where he lived and died. Opposed Bacon in his rebellion, but deserted by his troops. Married Mary ——; issue, among others:

CAPT. JOHN of Gloucester (d. 1720), Burgess, Councillor and County Lieutenant, and one of the founders of William and Mary College. Married, 1720, Elizabeth Cox (d. 1704, daughter of Henry and Arabella (Strachey) Cox; issue, among others, Mildred (b. April 1700), married Capt. Jno. Stubbs of Cappahosic, who was the ancestor of the writer.

## STRACHEY EXCURSUS.

WILLIAM, the immigrant, married, 1620, Eleanor Read, and had William (d. 1686), married ——; issue:

ARABELLA, married Henry Cox (d. 1674), and had Elizabeth (d. 1704), who married, 1690, Capt. Jno. Smith (d. 1720), who were the parents of MILDRED, who married Capt. John Stubbs of Cappahosic, Va.

## TALIAFERRO EXCURSUS.

ROBT. TALIAFERRO, "gentleman," of the "Borlase" family, of Cornwall, England, the immigrant (b. about 1635, d. about 1700), patented lands in Gloucester county, Virginia, 1655 and 1662, on Totapotomoy swamp running into Poropotank Creek. He, with Col. Lawrence Smith, patented 6,300 acres on the Rappahannock. Married Sarah, daughter of Rev. Charles Grymes of Gloucester county, Virginia. Issue:
   (1) Frances (d. 1716), married Elizabeth, daughter of Col. John Catlett of Essex county, Virginia. Issue:
   (a) John, of the "Mount;" (b) Robert, of Stafford; (c) William; (d) Richard; (e) Elizabeth, married Thos. Stribbling; (f) Agatha.
   (2) Lieut. Col. John (d. 1720, Burgess 1699), married 1682, Sarah, daughter Major Lawrence Smith; issue:
   (a) Capt. Lawrence, sheriff of Essex; married Sarah Thornton and was father of Wm. of King and Queen county, and grandfather of Philip of "Hockley."

(b) John, of Snow Creek, married Mary, daughter of Col. Jno. Catlett, Jr.

(c) Robert, married Elizabeth Mathews.

(d) Charles, married Mary ——.

(e) Zachariah.

(f) Catherine.

(g) Sarah.

(h) Mary.

(i) Elizabeth.

(j) Richard, married Elizabeth Eggleston, and had a daughter who married Chancellor Geo. Wythe.

(k) William.

(3)* Richard, of Richmond county, married Sarah ——, and has issue: (a) Richard; (b) Catherine; (c) Sarah; (d) Martha.

(4) Charles (d. 1726), married Mary ——; issue: Charles.

(5) Robert (d. 1688), married Sarah, daughter of Col. Jno. Catlett, and had issue:

(a) Robert (d. 1726).

(b) **Ann.**

(c) Elizabeth.

(6) Catherine, married Jno. Battaille.

Capt. Wm. Taliaferro, a son either of Francis or his brother, Lieut. Col. John, above, married Ann (b. 1707), daughter of James and Clara (Robinson) Walker of Urbanna, and had: (1) Wm. Walker, (2) Christopher, (3) Lucy, married (third wife) Charles Carter of Cleve, and was the mother of Ann Walker Carter, the ancestress of the writer.

## CATLETT EXCURSUS.

COL. JOHN CATLETT of Sittinburne, county Kent, **England,** received grants of land on Rappahannock in 1650. Presiding justice Rappahannock (now Essex) county. Killed by Indians in 1671 while defending Port Royal. He, with Edmund Scarborough and Richard Lawrence, were commissioners to settle boundaries between Virginia and Maryland in 1663. Married in 1657, Elizabeth Underwood (d. 1673), widow of Capt. Francis Slaughter, and had:

(I.) COL. JOHN (d. 1824), Burgess and presiding justice of Rappahannock (now Essex) county. Married Elizabeth Gaines; issue:

(1) Lawrence (d. 1724), married Alice Thornton. s. p.

(2) Elizabeth, married Rowland Thornton.

(3) John, of St. Mary's, parish Caroline (d. 1738), married Mary Grayson, and had:
  (a) John; (b) Mary; (c) Judith; (d) Elizabeth; (e) Benjamin; (f) Reuben; (g) William.

(4) Mary, married Jno. Taliaferro, of "Snow Creek."

(5) Thomas (d. 1739), married Martha ——, and had John of King William county (and perhaps others), who married (circa 1759) Mary Eggleston, sister to Richard Eggleston of Williamsburg, Va., and had:
  (a) John, of "Timberneck," a lawyer, who married, 1780, Ann Walker (b. 1764), daughter of Chas. and Lucy (Taliaferro) Carter of Cleve, and had:
    (*a*) Lucy Taliaferro Catlett, who married Capt. James Baytop of Springfield, the parents of the mother of the writer.
    (*b*) Matilda, married Christopher Morris (s. p.)
    (*c*) Henrietta, married Benj. Waller.
    (*d*) Martha, married first, Wm. Banks; second, Chas. Thruston.
    (*e*) Sarah, married Bartholomew Yates.
    (*f*) Mary, married Col. Robt. Thruston.
    (*g*) Ann, married Jno. Field.
    (*h*) John Walker Carter (b. 1803, d. 1883), of "Timberneck," lawyer and senator; married, first, Agnes Thruston; second, Fannie Burwell, and the father of Judge Charles and Landon Carter Catlett of Gloucester county, Virginia.

(6) Rebecca (d. 1760), married Francis Conway, and had a daughter, Eleanor Rose, who married, in 1749, Col. James Madison, and was the mother of President Madison.

(7) Margaret.

II. Sarah, married Robt. Taliaferro (d. 1688) and had issue.

III. Elizabeth (b, 1663), married Francis Taliaferro, and had issue.

IV. William (b. 1671, d. 1699), married Elizabeth Thompson; issue, a daughter, Elizabeth.

### CARTER EXCURSUS.

COL. JOHN CARTER (d. 1669), the immigrant, was son of Wm. Carter of the Inner Temple, Lord of the Manor of Gardstown in Hertfordshire, England. Settled first in Nansemond and then in

Lancaster county, Virginia. He was a burgess from both counties, councillor, and Colonel of the forces sent against the Indians. He married five times. By his wife Sarah Ludlow, he had:

ROBERT of Corotoman (b. 1663, d. 1732), often called "King" Carter. He was burgess, councillor, speaker, treasurer, governor and rector of William and Mary College. Married twice. By his first wife, Judith Armistead, had:

(1) John of "Shirley" married Elizabeth Hill, and was the ancestor of General Robt. E. Lee.

(2) Elizabeth, married, first, Nath. Burwell of Carter's Creek; second, Dr. Geo. Nicholas, and was the mother of Robert Carter Nicholas and an ancestor of the two governors by this name, and of Lewis Burwell, president of the Council.

(3) Judith, married Mann Page of Rosewell, and was the mother of Governor Page and ancestress of Mrs. T. Jefferson Stubbs, of Williamsburg, Va.

Robert married, second, Widow Willis, *nee* Bettie Landon, daughter of Thos. and Mary Landon; issue:

(4) Ann, married Benjamin Harrison of Berkeley, and was the ancestress of Presidents Wm. Henry and Benjamin Harrison.

(5) Robt. of Nomini, married Priscilla Bladon, and were parents of Robt., the councillor.

(6) Charles of Cleve (b. 1707, d. 1764), justice and burgess, married three times. By his last wife, Lucy Taliaferro, daughter of Capt. Wm. and Ann (Walker) Taliaferro, he had Ann Walker Carter, who married John Catlett of "Timberneck," and were the grandparents of Ann Walker Carter Baytop, the mother of the writer.

(7) Landon of Sabine Hall, married three times and left numerous descendants.

(8) Mary, married George Braxton of "Newington," and was the mother of Carter who signed the Declaration of Independence.

(9) Lucy, married Henry Fitzhugh, of "Eagle's Nest," the ancestress of Mrs. General Robt. E. Lee.

(10) George of Middle Temple, died s. p.

## LUDLOW EXCURSUS.

GABRIEL LUDLOW (b. 1587, d. 1639), the immigrant from Denton, England (the son of Thos., d. 1607, son of Geo., of Hill Deverill, sheriff of County Wiltz, 1567), came to Virginia and pat-

ented lands in Gloucester county, Virginia. He married ——,
and had Sarah, who married Col. Jno. Carter, and was the mother
of Robt. ("King") Carter, who was the grandfather of Ann
Walker Carter, the ancestress of the writer.

## LANDON EXCURSUS.

SILVANUS, of Credenhill, England, married, first, Anna, and
had:

(1) THOMAS, married Mary —— of Hereford county, Eng-
land, and was the father of Bettie, who married Robt.
("King") Carter.
Silvanus married, second, Frances, relict of Sir Anthony St.
Ledger, and had issue.

(2) SILVANUS; (3) MARY; (4) ANNE.
Thomas, above, was the immigrant, and came to Virginia and
settled in Middlesex county (where his will was probated, February 1701), after his union with Mary; issue:
(1) William, married Anne Jones of Pixley, Hereford, England; (2) Thomas; (3) Roger; (4) Silvanus (d. 1706);
(5) Rev. John.
(6) Mary (d. 1722), married, first, John Jones; second,
Alexander Swan (d. 1710).
(7) Ann, married, first, Wm. Ryfort; second, Rev. Thos.
Wheatland.
(8) St. Ledger.
(9) Elizabeth, married, first, Capt. Richard Willis; second,
Robert ("King") Carter, and was the grandmother of
Ann Walker Carter, who married John Catlett of Timberneck, great-grandfather of the writer.

## ROBINSON EXCURSUS.

CHRISTOPHER ROBINSON (b. 1645, d. 1693), son of John of
Cleasby, Yorkshire, England (and brother of Dr. Jno. Robinson,
Bishop of Bristol and London and Ambassador to Sweden, of
which country he wrote a history), settled in Middlesex county,
Virginia, in 1664, and named his home "Hewick,' after the old
family manor near Ripon in Yorkshire; burgess and councillor
and secretary of state. Married, first, Agatha (d. 1685), daughter of Bertram Obert; and second, 1687, Catherin Hone (d. 1692),
widow of Major Robt. Beverley and daughter of Maj. Theophilus
Hone (Burgess). Issue by first wife:

(1) Christopher (b. 1681, d. 1727), father of the Commissary.
(2) John (b. 1683, d. 1749), father of John the speaker.
(3) Agatha, died young.
(4) Ann, married Dr. John Hay (d. 1709).
(5) Elizabeth, died young (by second wife).
(6) Clara (b. 1689, d. 1715), married, in 1706, James Walker of Urbanna (d. 1720), the immigrant from Ashbourne in the Peak, Derbyshire, England.
(7) Theophilus, died young.
(8) Benjamin (sheriff of Essex, 1724).

James and Clara (Robinson) Walker had issue:

(1) Ann (b. 1707), married Capt. Wm. Taliaferro and had Walker, Christopher, and Lucy, who married, first, in 1762, Charles Carter of Cleve, and was mother of Ann Walker Carter, above, the ancestress of the writer. Lucy, married, second, Col. William Jones, and was ancestor of the Jones family of Gloucester county, Va.

(2) Jno. Walker (b. 1709, d. 1745), married, in 1733, Catherine, daughter of Bartholomew and Sarah (Mickleborough) Yates, and had Sarah (b. 1734), who married Robt. Page of Broad Neck. Their daughter Catherine married Benj. Carter Waller and was the ancestress of Mrs. Thos. Jefferson Stubbs of Williamsburg, Va.

### ROBINS EXCURSUS.

JOHN, Sr. and Jr., came to Virginia in 1622 on ship "Margaret and John," and patented 300 acres in Elizabeth City county, Virginia. John, Sr., went back to England, and on his return to Virginia in 1623, died at sea. John, Jr., patented "Robins' Neck" in Gloucester county in 1642, and lands on the Rappahannock in 1649. He was burgess 1646-49 for Elizabeth City county; also justice of the peace in 1642. Moved to Gloucester county just before his death in 1655. Married twice: first, Dorothy, and second Alice, and had three sons and two daughters:

(1) Christopher, the eldest son, married ——, and had Anne, who married Robt. Freeman; and Elizabeth, who married James Shackelford.
(2) William, died s. p.
(3) Dr. Thos., married, 1666, Mary Hansford, sister of Major Thos. Hansford of Bacon's Rebellion; issue: John, William, Thos. (s. p.), Richard, George and Benjamin.

Of the above only the descendants of John are known. He married Jane Throckmorton(?) and had Mary (b. 1693); Wm.

(b. 1715), and Albion. Albion had only daughters. Wm. married Elizabeth Coleman and had:

(1) John, d. s. p.

(2) Thomas, b. 1745, d. 1808; married, first, Frances Stubbs, daughter of Thomas and Mildred Stubbs, and had issue:

(a) Thos., married Ann Watkins Hudson; issue: Wm. David Simms; Thos. Coleman, who married Amelia Armistead, and had issue: William Augustine, and others; Robt. Coleman, Mrs. Heywood, Mrs. Luke, Mrs. Hagey, Mrs. Stubblefield, Mrs. Watlington, and Mrs. Dodson.

(b) Armistead of King William county, married Susan H. Pemberton, and had issue.

(c) Mrs. Chandler.

(d) Mrs. Borum.

(e) Mrs. Fitchett.

Married, second, Elizabeth Lee Hoomes:

(f) Dr. Joseph Hoomes, married Catherine Robins.

(g) Benj. Thos. Claiborne, married, first, Eliza T. Broadus; and second, Sarah Jane Maddox.

(3) Wm. (b. 1747, d. 1798), married, 1768, Dorothy Boswell (d. 1790); issue:

(a) Wm. (b. 1770, d. 1846), married, first, Eliza Whiting; second, Julianna Pryor; issue, Wm., no living issue. John married Eliza Thornton and had Richard Russell, Jno. W., and others. Augustine Warner (b. 1809, d. 1876), married Maria Todd and had Col. Wm. T. of Richmond, Va.; married, second, Elizabeth Todd, and had Mrs. Latane, Archie, Joseph, Taylor, and Mrs. Kemp.

(b) Elizabeth, married Jno. Stevens, and had issue.

(c) Anne, married Wm. Watlington.

(d) Susannah, married Frank Stubbs; no living issue.

(e) Rebecca, married James New Stubbs, and had Jeff. W. Stubbs, the father of the writer.

(4) Rebecca, married Isaac Singleton, and had issue.

(5) Elizabeth, married Jno. Stubbs, and had issue (see page 25).

(6) Jane, married Thos. Chamberlain, and had issue.

## Boswell Excursus.

Of this family little is known. Settling early in several counties and being of a roving disposition, it has been almost impossible to connect the numerous branches, of which only fragments are given below. The data given below, rather extensive in detail, may serve as a basis for future investigations.

SAMUEL BOSWELL, aged 23 years, came to Virginia in July, 1635. (Hotten.)

EDWARD BOSWELL, planter, paid his tax levy in Middlesex county (Lancaster), 1654. He was a vestryman of Lancaster parish, 1657, and took John Vause into partnership, 1658, on his plantation for twelve years. Christ Church register notes the "death of Mr. Boswells servants, 1661. In 1663, Edwin Boswell, 200 acres more in Gloucester county. (Va. Hist. Mag. V. 249.)

### Gloucester County Boswell.

FRANCIS BOSWELL (probably his brother) a patent in Gloucester (1656) "972 acres on north side of Ware river, adjoining the lands of Major Curtis." (Glo. Land Patents.)

10th June, 1666, THOMAS BOSWELL, 100 acres on north point of Ware riverside on to a small creek or gut on the point of a marsh of Ware point, including Raccoon island.

1676, DOROTHY BOSWELL was left a legacy in the will of Mathew Edwards, of Bruton parish, York county, "to be given her on her marriage day." (*York Records.*)

1682, THOMAS BOSWELL, 1100 acres on Timberneck creek, in Abingdon parish, extending a mile up from the mouth of the creek. (*Gloucester Patents.*)

1754, THOMAS BOSWELL, of Gloucester, lands in dispute between him and John Clayton, gent—(he the defendant)—survey began "in Mr. John Page's line and on to Mr. John Armistead's and to Jasper Clayton's tobacco ground." (*Old Survey Book.*)

1751, Petsworth parish indebted to Mr. THOMAS BOSWELL for serving a writ on Elizabeth Mills. (*Petsworth Vestry Book.*)

12th Aug. 1767, DOROTHY BOSWELL (d. March 17th, 1790) married William Robins of "Robins Neck" (b. Dec. 255, 1747, d. March 27, 1798), and believed to be the daughter of Thos. and Jane (Dunbar) Boswell; was the great-grandmother of the writer.

1767, THOMAS BOSWELL sold a tract of 423 acres in Kingston, parish.

1768, CAPT. THOMAS BOSWELL had a lottery at Gloucester Court House to pay his debts. The *managers* were Thomas and Francis Whiting, Col. Francis Tomkies, Jasper Clayton and David Kerr, to which lottery John Clayton protested, saying that "the 4 slaves offered as the prizes had been conveyed to him by the *late*

*Thomas Boswell"* (father of Capt. Thomas?) His claims were paid. The wife of Capt. Thomas Boswell was probably a Machen of an old Middlesex county family. They had at least two children: Dr. Machen, and Jane, who married, first, —— Thornton, and second, John Seawell, and probably also Molly, who married (1775) Churchill Armistead. Old Chancery papers mention "Col. Machen Boswell as administrator of Thomas Boswell, dec'd." Maj. Thomas Boswell was in the Virginia State Line during the Revolution. (*Hening,* II., 311.)

Dr. MACHEN BOSWELL, will 1793, p. 1794, by Mann Page and Francis Whiting, executors: Ben Dabney of King and Queen, and John Seawell of Gloucester; children: 1, Thomas; 2, Elizabeth, married, first, 1805, Ralph Wormeley, second, Carter M. Braxton; 3, Martha, married Mr. Roy.

1752. JOHN BOSWELL owned lands on Ware river, when Jane Boswell of London made Capt. Gwyn Reade her attorney for her lands in Gloucester—a part of 400 acres. The land ran up Ware river and was on Jefferson's creek and near to Mordecai Booth and Richard Ransom—218 acres of which belonged to John Boswell.

1754. THOMAS and BENJAMIN BOSWELL lands surveyed. (*Old Survey Book.*)

1767. GEORGE BOSWELL sold a tract in Ware Neck, North river, 300 acres "almost surrounded by a creek, so as to need but little fencing;" and also, in 1770, a survey for him by Francis Tomkies of 270 acres on North river, and Back creek in Ware Neck.

*Boswell—(Abingdon Parish Register, Gloucester County.)*

Mary, daughter of Elizabeth Boswell (b. Jan. 15th, 1685).
Roger, son of Elizabeth Boswell (b. April 29th, 1688).
Richard, son of Elizabeth Boswell (b. March 30th, 1690).
John, son of John and Phoebe Boswell (b. March 5th, 1692).
Robert, son of John and Phoebe Boswell (b. Sept. 18th, 1698).
Joseph, son of John and Phoebe Boswell (b. March 26th, 1700).
Diana, daughter of John and Phoebe Boswell (b. Oct. 10th, 1701).
Mary, daughter of John and Phoebe Boswell (b. Jan. 3d, 1703).
Joseph Boswell, married Oct. 23d, 1731, Jane Shackelford. Their son Benjamin was born July 23d, 1732.

*From Kingston Register, Gloucester County (now Mathews.)*

Pangranparaba Boswell, married January 1756, Sarah Young.
John, son of above, born Nov. 10th, 1756.

John Boswell of Gloucester county, married Ann, daughter of
Charles Nuttall of Gloucester and sister of Wm. and John Nuttall of the Revolutionary Army. Their son George William
Frederick Boswell (b. 1791), married his cousin, Ann New Nuttall, daughter of John. All moved to North Carolina.

Iverson Jacobs Boswell of Gloucester county, married a daughter of Reuben Davis, who inherited, in 1806, lands from her
father's estate. (*Old Surveys.*)

Abraham Iverson was Justice in Gloucester, 1681. Gregory
and Richard Iverson, in Gloucester 1752.

John Boswell, son and heir of David Boswell, sold lands in
New Kent (jointly with Robert Booth) to the father of Francis
Page, who in his will, 1694, mentions the transaction. (*Page
Book* 44.)

John Boswell of St. George parish, Hanover, will probated
April, 1741; eldest daughter, Dorothy; youngest, Frances; sons,
Ransom, John, George and James. "The rest of his estate for
instruction and education of his youngest children and desired the
court to bind at their ages Ransom and John to a joyner, and
George to a blacksmith." Wife, Ann ——.

Maj. John Boswell of Hanover, 1765, helped furnish provisions
to the army (*Hening,* VIII., 181) and the *Virginia Gazette* mentions him, 1768.

Capt. William Boswell married in Elizabeth City, March 2d,
1702, Ellinor, widow of Coleman Brough. Their daughter,
Grace Boswell, was the third wife of John Selden, who was Justice in Elizabeth City, 1725, and Deputy King's Attorney, 1752.

Ellinor Boswell, married, second, 1727, in Elizabeth City,
George Yeo, who in his will (1742) left legacies to the children
of John and Grace Selden, calling them "children of my said
cousin (nephew) Selden." John Selden his executor. (*Wm.
and Mary Quarterly,* V., 61.)

William Boswell of Mathews county, student at William and
Mary College, 1811.

"John Iverson Boswell of the Revolution (d. March 3d, 1823)
had a son, John Iverson, Jr.,* who died Dec. 15, 1846. He made
a family register, from the old records, Sept. 24, 1817. His
brother, Wm. Washington Boswell of Henrico county, owned the
family Bible, now in possession (1902) of Miss Hannah Boswell,
living with Dr. Joseph Boswell at Chase City, Macklenburg
county, Virginia.

John Iverson Boswell, Sr., born April 5th, 1761, in Gloucester county(?), married, first, in March, 1784, Mary ———, and second, Oct. 27th, 1797, Barbara Walker.  Issue:

(1)  Eliza (b. Nov. 28th, 1784).
(2)  Joseph (b. Sept. 3d, 1786), father of Dr. Joseph of Chase City, Mecklenberg county.
(3)  Thomas (b. May 26th, 1788, d. Sept. 18, 1791).
(4)  Charity (b. April 20th, 1790, d. Sept. 15th, 1791).
(5)  Ann (b. March 11th, 1792).
(6)  Mary (b. Feb. 26th, 1794, d. Nov. 6, 1805).
(7)  *John Iverson, Jr. (b. Jan. 23d, 1796, d. Dec. 15, 1846).
(8)  Charity (b. Oct. 28th, 1798).
(9)  William Washington (b. April 13th, 1801), of Henrico county.
(10)  Susan (b. March 11th, 1803).
(11)  Lucy (b. Nov. 1, 1805).
(12)  Mary (b. May 4th, 1808).
(13)  Martha (b. July 3d, 1811).

*John Iverson Boswell, Jr., above (b. 1796), married Nov. 29th, 1818, first, Nancy D. Coleman (b. Feb. 7th, 1801, d. May 29th, 1834), and married, second, Dec. 18th, 1838, Ellen J. Somerville.  Issue: (1) Sarah A., b. 1819; (2) Joseph C., b. 1820; (3) Mary L., b. 1821, d. 1821; (4) Edwin S., b. 1824, d. 1826; (5) Henry I., b. 1826; (6) John L., b. 1829; (7) Lewellyn, b. 1832; (8) Lewis A., b. 1834; (9) Mary E., b. 1840; (10) Edmund D., b. 1841; (11) Thomas R., b. 1843; (12) William W., b. 1845.

"Murdered in the Southampton insurrection, 1831, Mrs. C. Whitehead, three daughters, two sons and one grandson."  This is believed to have been Charity Boswell, given above.

1658—Thomas Boswell, 800 acres on the Potomac river; and in 1664 these lands, now 972 acres, renewed in name of his son, Thomas Boswell.

1690—John Boswell, witness will in Perquimans county, North Carolina.

1735—Will of Wm. Boswell, who married Margaret Nicholson, mentions wife and following children: Thos., John, Ichabod and Mary; recorded in State Office, Raleigh, N. C.

1741—Will of Geo. Boswell of Perquimans county, North Carolina, mentions children: Geo., Isaac, and Isabel.

1757—John and Joseph Boswell witness wills in Perquimans county, North Carolina.

## COLEMAN EXCURSUS.

From the Land Books at Richmond, Richard Coleman patented in 1654, 1400 acres and 600 acres on Rappahannock. In 1663, Wm. Coleman and Robt. Baynham, 300 acres in Lancaster county. In 1666, Robt. Coleman, 110 acres; in 1667, 300 acres. In 1667, Robt. Coleman, 600 acres in Isle of Wight, of which he was a headright. In 1667, Robt. Coleman, Sr., 283 acres on Rappahannock river. In 1667, Robt. Coleman and Wm. Ruffin, 184 acres in Isle of Wight.

In 1748, an old survey of Gloucester county, Robt. and Joseph and Ellis Coleman owned lands adjoining Lawrence Smith's lands.

In Abingdon Parish Records occur the following:

Ann, daughter of Thos. and Rebekah Coleman (b. July 3d, 1680).

Grisell, daughter of Thos. and Rebekah Coleman (b. April 30th, 1682).

Rebecca, daughter of Thos. and Rebekah Coleman (b. Jan. 20th, 1684).

Sarah, daughter of Thos. and Rebekah Coleman (b. June 6th, 1686).

Thomas, son of Thos. and Rebekah Coleman (b. Feb. 7th, 1688).

Mary, daughter of Thos. and Rebekah Coleman (b. Oct. 10th, 1689).

John, son of Thos. and Rebekah Coleman (b. March, 1699).

Robt., son of Thos. and Rebekah Coleman (b. Feb. 20th, 1701).

John, son of Joseph and Agnes Coleman (b. April 10th, 1680).

Adbeston, son of Joseph and Agnes Coleman (b. Dec. 8th, 1689).

James, son of John and Margaret Coleman (b. Aug. 30th, 1693).

Robert, son of Thos. Coleman (b. Dec. 6th, 1713).

Joseph, son of Thos. and Elizabeth Coleman (b. Feb. 16th, 1715).

Rebecca, daughter of Thos. and Elizabeth Coleman, (b. March 5th, 1718).

Elizabeth, daughter of Thos. and Elizabeth Coleman (b. April 3d, 1721).

Thomas, son of Thos. and Elizabeth Coleman (b. July 5th, 1722).

Mary, daughter of Thos. and Elizabeth Coleman (b. Aug. 5th, 1726).

A daughter of Thos. and Elizabeth Coleman (b. Feb. 2d, 1728).

Rachel, a daughter of Thos. and Elizabeth Coleman (b. May 24th, 1730).

Diana, daughter of Thos. and Elizabeth Coleman (b. Feb. 5th, 1732).

Susannah, daughter of Thos. and Elizabeth Coleman (b. Jan. 16th, 1736).

John, son of Thos. and Elizabeth Coleman (b. Oct. 15th, 1758).

Richard, son of John Coleman (b. Sept. 1st, 1723).

Joseph, son of John Coleman (b. Sept. 12th, 1725).

James, son of John Coleman and wife (b. Dec. 5th, 1732).

John, son of John and Grace Coleman (b. Sept. 17th, 1726).

Jno., son of James and Elizabeth Coleman (b. Feb. 4th, 1722).

Sarah, daughter of Joseph and Grace Coleman (b. May 19th, 1757, d. Nov. 30th, 1759),

Jno., son of Richard and Hannah Coleman (b. Dec. 27th, 1737).

Jane, son of Joseph and Rebecca Coleman (b. Nov. 5th, 1740).

Elizabeth, daughter of Joseph and Rebecca Coleman (b. May 10th, 1743).

Rebecca, daughter of Joseph and Rebecca Coleman (b. Oct. 14th, 1744).

Thomas, son of Joseph and Rebecca Coleman (b. May 4th, 1746).

Mary, daughter of James and Sarah Coleman (b. Dec. 15th, 1754).

Richard, son of James and Sarah Coleman (b. Jan. 18th, 1761).

John, son of James and Sarah Coleman (b. April 7th, 1757).

Thomas, son of Richard and Johanna Coleman (b. Nov. 20th, 1743).

George, son of Richard and Johanna Coleman (b. Sept. 1743).

Robt., son of Rebt. and Elizabeth Coleman (b. Nov. 1st, 1746).

Elizabeth, daughter of Robt. and Elizabeth Coleman (b. Oct. 25th, 1749).

Whitley, son of Robt. and Elizabeth Coleman (b. Nov. 8th, 1751, d. 1752).

In the Petsworth Parish Book, Jno. (1695), Samuel (1729), Richard (1784), Joseph (1701), and Mrs. Ann Coleman (1711), names occur. Jno. Coleman was vestryman in 1708.

The marriages in Abingdon Parish Records are as follows:

Wm. Robins married Elizabeth Coleman, Dec. 1st, 1737.

Jno. Hall married Rebecca Coleman, Aug. 3d, 1745.

Joseph Ryland married Sarah Coleman, Feb. 21st, 1741.

The deaths recorded in same Records are:

Sarah, daughter of Joseph Coleman, died October, 1759.

Mrs. Grace Coleman, died Jan. 19th, 1758.

Grace Coleman, died Nov. 30th, 1757.

Mrs. Elizabeth Coleman, died May 12th, 1751.

The will of Robt. Coleman of Essex, probated 1734, mentions: wife, Ann; sons, Thomas, Robert and Edward; daughters, Ann, Elizabeth and Grisett Chamberlin.

A record of births of 18 slaves are also recorded in Abingdon to the following: Hannah, John, Richard, Elizabeth and Joseph Coleman, from 1738 to 1757.

An inspection of above records will show Thomas, Joseph and James were living in 1701, and with Robert of Essex are presumably brothers and sons of the immigrant to Gloucester.

Thos. and Rebecca Coleman had a son, Thomas, who married Elizabeth ——, and had Elizabeth Coleman, who married Wm. Robins in 1737, and was the ancestress of the writer and of the Robinses of Gloucester county, Virginia.

Thos. and Rebecca Coleman had also John, who married Grace, and had James, who married Sarah ——. and had Richard (b. 1761), member of Capt. Nath. Welch's Co., 2d Va. Regt., Col. Wm. Brent, and was honorably discharged in 1780, after severe service in Philadelphia. Kiskiatt, Ramapage, Lancaster and Mendeham. He married Ann Stubbs and was the ancestor of the Colemans of Gloucester county, Virginia.

### HANSFORD EXCURSUS.

John, will probated 1661, of York county, Virginia, married Elizabeth ——, who married, second, Edward Lockey (d. 1667). Issue by first marriage (none by second):

    (1) Maj. Thomas of Bacon's Rebellion, of age 1666, hung by order Sir Wm. Berkley; married Elizabeth Jones, daughter of Richard Jones, deceased.

    (2) Chas., married Elizabeth, widow of Joseph Moody (d. 1679), *nee* Foliott.

    (3) John (d. before 1675).

    (4) William.

    (5) Elizabeth, married, first, Christian Wilson; second, Randolph Holt of Surry.

    (6) Mary, married Dr. Thos. Robins of Robins Neck, Gloucester county, Virginia, and was the ancestress of all the Robinses in Gloucester county, Virginia.

Richard, brother of above John, patents, in 1650, lands in York county.

John also patents lands in 1658 in York county, and in 1653, lands in Gloucester, among the latter, "Clay Bank," which he leaves to his sons, John and William.

## New Excursus.

It is to be regretted that so little data of this family has been collected. Only a few fragments can, therefore, be presented.

EDWARD NEW, of Charles City county, Virginia, married Sarah, daughter of Edward Bland (son of John of London, will 1680). They had a son, JOHN NEW, living in 1752. (Hening. VI., p. 313).

There were News and Duvals in Henrico county, Virginia, in 1771.

THOMAS NEW and FRANCIS NEW, a deed made by them and Phoebe Booth, 1680.

THOMAS NEW, deputy clerk, Essex county, Virginia, 1685.

JAMES and SAMUEL NEW, on the Savannah river, Georgia, 1754.

It is probable that the JAMES NEW mentioned in an old survey of Ware parish, in 1754, was the father of the following:

I. DANIEL NEW, clerk of Petsworth Church, 1739-1758; will 1775, probated 1776, mentions children:
  (1) Daniel, married daughter of Wm. Duval (d. 1785), and had James and Carter (and three or four daughters), members of vestry, Petsworth parish, 1777.
  (2) Jno. New, kept ordinary at Gloucester Court House, and in 1776 was thanked by Capt. Joseph Spencer of 2nd Va., for kindness when they marched to Gwynn's Island. (*Virginia Gazette,* 1776.) He married ——, and had James, John, Annie and Pattie.
  (3) Martha New, married, first, Guthrie; and second, Dulier; issue, Aphia, who married Henry Enos and had issue.
  (4) Sarah New, married Wm. Shackelford (d. s. p.)
  (5) Elizabeth New, married —— Garland.

II. ELIZABETH NEW (d. 1778), married circa 1760, Wm. Stubbs, and had James New Stubbs, the grandfather of the writer.

III. ANTHONY NEW (b. 1747 in Gloucester county, Virginia), removed to Caroline county. Member House of Delegates 1787. Member of Congress from December 1793 to March 1805. Removed to Elkton, Ky. Member of Congress from Kentucky in 12th, 15th and 17th Congresses. Died March 2d, 1833. Married Nancy Wiatt of Caroline county, Virginia, and had (1) Anthony, who remained in Virginia and married Ann S. Bracken, and had Fannie Bracken New, who married John Carnes Cooke. (See Cooke Pamphlet.)

Emanuel Jones Thruston in 1820 administered the estates of Anthony New and his wife, Ann S. (Bracken) New. He was also the guardian of Fannie Bracken New, who married John Carnes Cooke.

A daughter of Anthony and Nancy (Wiatt) New married —— Starke of Norfolk, and was the mother of L. D. Starke, member of the law firm of Starke & Starke, Norfolk, Va. (1895).

# ACKNOWLEDGMENTS.

The writer is indebted to the following for Bible records, family histories, and other valuable information:

Mrs. S. J. Hudgins, Richmond, Va.
Hon. Jno. R. Saunders, Urbanna, Va.
Thos. Reade Purcell, Gloucester, Va.
Richard Taliaferro, Gloucester, Va.
Richard C. Coleman, Gloucester, Va.
George D. Stubbs, Gloucester, Va.
Dr. T. Jefferson Stubbs, Williamsburg, Va.
Mrs. Tallulah L. Gachet, Auburn, Ala. (d. 1900).
Mrs. M. S. Mathenay, Utica, Miss.
Miss Sallie Stubbs, Memphis, Tenn.
Mrs. Sarah E. Gray, Allen, Texas.
Col. Frank P. Stubbs, Monroe, La.
Miss Kate Palmer Stubbs, Delta, La.
Mrs. Fannie J. Chestney, Macon, Ga.
Hon. Edwin F. Jones, Montgomery, Ala.
Hon. James Baytop Stubbs, Galveston, Texas.
Mrs. Mary Ann Hannon, Montgomery, Ala. (d. 1898).
Edward Baytop Stubbs, Bessemer, Ala.
Robt. E. McKinney, Henderson, Tenn.
Capt. John Smith Stubbs, Cedarton, Ga.
Wm. L. Wilson, Maude, Ga.
Mrs. Stephen Collins, Fairburn, Ga.
James Arnold Stubbs, Fairburn, Ga.
Mrs. Fannie S. Brown, Bremen, Ga.
John W. Stubbs, Pine Log, Ga.
Prof. C. O. Stubbs, Westminster, Texas.
J. S. Weems, Sanders, Ga.
Mrs. E. L. Linch, Linchburg, Ga.
Mrs. J. R. Ammons, Bonaire, Ga.
Mrs. J. A. Hunt, Abbeville, Ga.
Mrs. F. F. Farmer, Abbeville, Ga.
Mrs. Eugenia C. Stubbs, Cairo, Ga.
Mrs. Martha F. Moreland, Americus, Ga.
Rev. Thos. W. Darley, Quitman, Ga.
Peter Woodward Stubbs, Tobesofkee, Ga.
Mrs. M. Josephine King, Atlanta, Ga.
Mrs. Ida King, Atlanta, Ga.
Mrs. Maude S. Pritchett, Dublin, Ga.

Thomas M. Stubbs, Blanco, Texas.
Mrs. Rebecca Dozier Stubbs, Franklin, Tenn.
Mrs. Eudora Sawyer, Galveston, Texas.
Rev. Geo. G. Smith, Macon, Ga.
Dennis Dokes, Lightfoot, Ga.
Sidney Johnson Stubbs, Macon, Ga.
Wm. B. Stubbs, Savannah, Ga.
Mrs. M. A. Pittman, Abbeville, Ga.
Amariah Biggs Stubbs, Arguta, Ala.
Mrs. Dr. T. L. Jenkins, Chipley, Ga.
Frank M. Stubbs, Augusta, Ga.
Archibald McNeal Stubbs, Nathaniel, Ga.
Robt. Davis Stubbs, Eatonton, Ga.
Hon. J. J. Stubbs, Raleigh, Miss.
Hon. Henry W. Stubbs, Williamston, N. C.
C. E. Stubbs, Sumter, S. C.
Dr. Robert Armistead Stewart, University of Virginia.